The Foods of Italy

AN ENDLESS ADVENTURE IN TASTE

by Burton Anderson

Italian Trade Commission
Trade Promotion Section of the
Consulate General of Italy

The Foods of Italy

Published by: The Italian Trade Commission
33 East 67th Street - New York, NY 10065

© 2008 Italian Trade Commission - 4th Edition

Table of Contents

Greetings from Aniello Musella
Italian Trade Commissioner - Executive Director for the USA

Dear Reader,

I am pleased to invite you to explore the cuisine of Italy and learn more about its palatable regional bounties from this new edition of The Foods of Italy.

Traditionally in Italy, we have always demanded that those entrusted with carrying on the rich culture and gastronomic traditions indigenous to our diverse territories, make every effort to bring forth their best in quality, innovation, style and variety.

As geography, climate, terroir and culinary history vary from North to South, so do the distinct regional delicacies. Still, in a world driven by mass culture, fast food and uniform tastes, Italian food producers have remained refreshingly loyal to our unique local traditions and products which have been improved by the introduction of the latest methods of agriculture and food processing.

We are pleased that the United States remains one of the top importers of Italian food and wine in the world. Americans have certainly become familiar with the variety of quality Italian food products and the health benefits associated with their consumption. Consequently, more Americans have chosen to introduce a taste of Italy into their daily lives by buying and cooking with savory authentic Italian products. Today, more American consumers are starting to recognize the stark difference between the plethora of imitation Italian products flooding the US market and the authentic high quality Italian delicacies available.

This phenomenon is spreading across the nation and is no longer limited to America's coasts. Restaurants specializing in Italian cuisine have sprung up in communities throughout the United States and their number continues to grow at an astonishing rate. Restaurants that are not specifically committed to Italian cooking have started to incorporate authentic Italian ingredients into their dishes. In recent years, more super markets and other mass merchandising outlets have been trying to satiate the consumer demand by offering a growing selection of imported authentic Italian food. We are encouraged by these observations which have been backed up by official government data substantiating America's appreciation of Italian food and wines.

I sincerely hope that you will enjoy this volume and that you will make it a favorite part of your home library. I also invite you to visit our website www.italianmade.com which is constantly being updated and contains the latest news about the foods and wines of Italy.

Sincerely yours,

Italy, Where Eating is an Art

The Italian way of eating exalts the genius of a people who pride themselves on artistic self expression in drawing from the assets of a land that is intricately diverse by nature. Human and natural elements have combined in kitchens over time to engender an astonishing variety of dishes. That explains why la cucina italiana does not represent a national way of cooking so much as an encyclopedic fund of recipes, techniques and flavors of local inspiration.

Italian food has triumphed at all levels around the world, in temples of gourmet dining as well as in cafés, pizza parlors, wine bars, fancy food shops, supermarkets and corner groceries. Popularity has led to widespread imitation, often in the form of respectful emulation among chefs in many lands who rely on Italian concepts of cooking to fashion menus with a Mediterranean accent. But the vogue of eating Italian style has also led to exploitation of stereotypes that favor mass production and standardization of tastes.

Travelers in Italy note that wherever you go you dine not only well but differently. Each region, province, town and village has its repertoire of traditional foods and dishes that rely on local ingredients.

Traditions have evolved with time to take into account the wider range of available foods and new methods of preparing them. Italian chefs can be as style conscious as any, creating dishes that reflect modern concepts of taste. Yet it's interesting to note that major trends in dining in Italy reflect a return to the past, drawing on the traditions of the family trattoria and the neighborhood osteria.

Equally significant is the tendency to favor natural foods. Italy is Europe's leading producer of organically grown produce, or what is known as cibo biologico raised or processed without the use of chemical pesticides, herbicides and fertilizers.

Fresh produce is essential to Italian cooks, with their knack for making things look easy. But menus also rely on specialty foods—cheeses, pastas, cured meats, seafood, baked goods, extra virgin olive oil, vinegars, condiments and sauces—crafted by artisans following age-old techniques.

Italians trace their gastronomic heritage to Romans, Greeks, Etruscans, Arabs and other Mediterranean peoples who elaborated the methods of raising, refining and preserving foods. But dining customs acquired local accents in a land divided by mountains and seas into natural enclaves where independent spirits developed during the repeated shifts of ruling powers that fragmented Italy from Roman times to the Risorgimento.

Still, despite the different attitudes about eating expressed from the Mediterranean isles to the Alps, Italian foods have points in common. Consider pizza, which migrated from Naples to become what must rank as Italy's—and the world's—favorite fast food. Every Italian town has a gelateria making ice cream, sherbet and shaved ice granita. And every piazza has a bar or two where tiny cups of densely aromatic espresso are brewed rigorously to command.

Pasta is a national institution, though noodles and the like come in so many shapes and sizes and carry so many names that there is no way of documenting them all. Still, pasta falls into two basic categories: the dried, made from hard wheat semola meal and water, and the fresh, made from soft wheat flour, usually with eggs and often with other ingredients in the dough or filling.

Dried pasta prevailed in the south and fresh pasta in the north, in territories similar to those long described as "the Italy of olive oil and the Italy of butter." But barriers fell as spaghetti and maccheroni gained ground in the Alps and beyond while ravioli and tortellini (with their northern partners risotto and polenta) won admirers in the Mezzogiorno. Meanwhile, extra virgin olive oil has continued to triumph everywhere as the essence of the Mediterranean diet.

Each province of Italy has its own salumi-cured meats, usually from pork but also from other animals, in the forms of prosciutto, salame, sausages, mortadella, bresaola and more. Italians produce an extraordinary range of cheeses. The best known is Parmigiano-Reggiano®, or Parmesan, used universally for grating but savored at home in bite-sized chunks. Grana Padano, Gorgonzola, Fontina, Provolone, Caciacavallo, Pecorino Romano and Sardo also have international followings, as does the mozzarella melted over pizza but also eaten fresh. Yet most Italian formaggio remains proudly local.

The same can be said for breads, which range in type from hefty loaves of unsalted pane toscano to Emilia's tawny coppiette rolls to Alto Adige's dark rye Bauernbrot to Turin's stick-like grissini to Sardinia's thin, crisp, brittle bread carta da musica and on through a nationwide assortment of flatbreads or focacce. The inventory of pastries, biscuits, cakes, chocolates and other types of sweets is equally awe inspiring.

Italian meals may progress through multiple courses, from antipasto to primo and secondo, formaggio, frutta and on to dolce. But even a simple repast would not be complete without vino in the country that produces the greatest variety of types and styles of wine.

Italy, with a population of about 57 million, consists of 20 regions subdivided into 103 provinces that take the names of prominent towns. Each province boasts distinctive foods and wines, which, needless to say, have an inherent affinity for one another. Today, in a world of ever more uniform tastes, Italians retain their customary loyalty to local foods and wines.

The following pages provide an account of Italian food through the ages, a review of specialty foods made in the country, a discussion of dining customs and the types of eating and drinking places to be found in Italy. At the end is a glossary with definitions of commonly used terms for foods and beverages.

The main part of the volume is a region-by-region survey of foods and styles of cooking. It begins in the south, in those antique Mediterranean lands where the roots of Italy's culinary culture took form, and moves up the peninsula past Rome and Florence and over the Apennines to the Po valley, the nation's most abundant source of produce, to conclude at the northern border of the Alps. Hundreds of special foods and dishes are described, though accounts are by no means exhaustive.

Italian Food Through the Ages

Ancient Rome gave western civilization the foundations of sophisticated cuisine. Yet, while building their empire, the Romans gathered as many culinary secrets as they propagated. Other Mediterranean peoples—including Etruscans and early Italians whose accomplishments are rarely acknowledged—already knew the skills of milling cereals and leavening flour for bread, crushing olives for oil, converting milk to cheese and grapes to wine and vinegar.

The diets of some contemporaries were more appetizing than the fare of the early Romans, who subsisted mainly on millet or spelt porridge called puls, ewe's milk whey cheeses, primitive wines and what they could scavenge from woods, fields and streams. The Greeks ate and drank so well in their southern Italian colonies of Magna Graecia that Archestratus became known as the father of gastronomy for his ode to the foods of Sicily in the third century B.C.

Over time, though, Romans elevated agriculture from a rudimentary craft to a science, while advancing methods of preparing, preserving and shipping provisions. They developed a thriving trade in wine, grains, and salt, so valued as a flavoring and agent for curing foods (especially pork as salume) that soldiers were paid salaries with it. What the Romans lacked, they imported, introducing exotic varieties of poultry, fruits, vegetables, grains and spices that eventually became standard Italian fare.

The culinary heritage of Imperial Rome was documented by Apicius (who may have been more than one person) in De Re Coquinaria, the original cookbook. It described a remarkable range of vegetable, meat and seafood dishes, uses of mushrooms, truffles, fruits, nuts, cheeses, breads, cakes and wines. Recipes revealed a fondness for herbs and spices, heavy use of a potent sauce called garum based on rancid fish entrails and a taste for sweet-sour, which, in the absence of refined sugar relied in part on honey and grape juice cooked down as syrup.

Memories of Romans as sybarites and gluttons can be blamed on the extravagant feasts of certain rulers and the collective excesses of the bourgeoisie of a declining empire. Through most of their long history, however, Romans exercised moderation in a diet based on simple and wholesome Mediterranean foods.

People of later eras weren't always so lucky. During the Dark Ages, most Italians could only dream of feasting while facing the daily challenge of getting enough to eat. Their homeland was overrun by barbarians, who had a habit of devouring anything edible they could pillage. Eventually, though, some foreigners contributed new foods. The Arabs, who occupied southern Italy in the 9th century, brought cane sugar,

9

spices, raisins and candied fruits that set the lasting styles for sweets and ices in the Mezzogiorno.

The origins of pasta in Italy had been credited to sources ranging over time from the ancient Greeks to Marco Polo, who returned to Venice with noodles from the Orient in the late 13th century. But the first documented evidence of a pasta industry was attributed to Arabs in 12th century Sicily. From there the cult spread gradually through the south (where dried maccheroni and spaghetti have always prevailed) and on to points north (where eggs were often used in dough for fresh pasta noodles and stuffed envelopes).

Before the advent of pasta, generations of Italians used grains or chestnuts or chickpea pastes for breads, cakes, dumplings, polenta-like mushes and gruels. Flatbreads acquired toppings long before Neapolitans came up with the pizza that went on to conquer the world.

Diets improved in the late Middle Ages, with the growing prosperity of city-states and the arrival of edibles from other places. Venetian, Genoese and Pisan traders distributed choice goods around Italy, while introducing Mediterranean flavors to northern Europe. With spices from the east came rice, which proved more productive than other grains of the time, though only in recent eras did Po valley dwellers light upon the secrets of risotto.

The Renaissance uplifted the culinary arts, evident in the banquets of Rome's papal court, the Venice of the doges and perhaps most elegantly in the Florence of the Medici. That family's epicurean tastes were transferred to France when Caterina de' Medici wed King Henry II, bringing with her the cooks and recipes that reputedly put the haute in cuisine.

But perhaps the most significant Italian contribution to European cooking, if indirect, was Christopher Columbus's discovery of America. In the centuries that followed, the New World endowed the Old with the potato, beans, squash, novel breeds of fowl, chili peppers, corn for northern Italy's massively popular polenta and, above all, the tomato, which after posing for a time as an ornamental plant burst forth in the south in the most Italian of sauces.

Italians have a knack for making plants thrive in their Mediterranean climate, but even things that don't grow have reached new heights in their hands. Consider coffee, imported from the tropics since Venetians introduced the raw beans to Italy in the 1600s, but elevated to the sublime in this century through the ingenious roasting, blending and steam pressure processing of espresso.

After ages of foreign domination had fragmented Italy, the country pieced itself back together in the Risorgimento with a new spirit of unity that inspired notions of a national cuisine. The chief advocate was Pellegrino Artusi, whose La scienza in cucina e l'arte di mangiar bene, first published in 1891, collected nearly 800 recipes from around the country. That was no small feat, since Italian cooks have always relied more on personal tastes and intuition than written recipes with precise measures and steps. But today, despite attempts to standardize cooking from the Alps to the Mediterranean isles, la cucina italiana stands as a model of diversity to be savored in the proudly traditional dishes of each region.

Italian Specialty Foods

Italy's wealth of gastronomic treasures attests to the wisdom and skill of generations of artisans who have kept alive their ancestral heritage of taste. The following specialty foods and beverages are made following standards of excellence that are uniquely Italian.

Olio extra vergine di oliva (extra virgin olive oil). Italy, which produces nearly a third of the world's olive oil, is distinguished by the superior class of its extra vergine, made in all regions of the center and south and in a few places in the north. The most flavorful and wholesome of comestible oils is used raw in dressings or sauces for salads, vegetables, pastas, soups, seafood and meats, though chefs find extra vergine unmatchable in cooking, despite the higher cost. The best oils show distinct character due to terrain and climate, the varieties of olives they come from and methods of harvesting. Hand picking of under-ripe olives renders oil of deep green color, fruity aroma and full flavor (sometimes a touch piquant). Mature olives make oil of paler color and subtler flavor. Traditional extraction by stone crushing and mat pressing is practiced occasionally in mills in Tuscany and Umbria, where oil is especially prized, though most is processed by mechanical mashing and centrifuging. By law, olio extra vergine di oliva must come from the first pressing of olives by mechanical (not chemical) means and must contain less than 1 percent of oleic acid (the key measure: the lower the acidity the better). Olio vergine di oliva may have a maximum of 2 percent acidity; what is called simply olio di oliva may be rectified and deacidified. Italy has established zones of protected origin (DOP) where extra vergine oils carry a geographical name. Such oils are usually best within a year of the harvest, since flavor slowly fades. Italy is also a major producer and exporter of table olives.

Formaggio (cheese). Italians produce more than 450 different types of cheese, some renowned, others local rarities. In the north, cow's milk cheeses prevail, led by the grana family of Parmigiano-Reggiano® (Parmesan) and Grana Padano, which together account for a third of Italy's formaggio. Those firm cheeses, of granular texture, are used for grating, though they are often more appreciated in bite-sized morsels. Other popular northern cheeses are blue-veined Gorgonzola, creamy Fontina, Taleggio, Asiago, Stracchino and Robiola. In central and southern Italy, cheese from sheep's milk is called pecorino, distinguished as Romano, Sardo (Sardinian) and Toscano (Tuscan). Southern Italians make a variety of pasta filata cheeses, worked into strands before taking form. The spongy mozzarella is best from the milk of water buffalo. Caciocavallo and Provolone are aged and sometimes smoked. Goat's milk cheese made in various places is called caprino. Popular everywhere in Italy are soft cooked whey called ricotta and lightly fermented cream called mascarpone.

Pasta. The category of pasta alimentare covers noodles and the like in myriad forms and sizes, produced, flavored, dressed and served in infinite ways. Categories of pasta are confused by the fact that names of similar types vary from place to place and that different types may carry the same name. Pasta secca (dry) is made primarily from coarse durum wheat flour and water into dough shaped mechanically by being forced through slots of varying sizes and patterns and cut and dried. Pasta secca may be divided as lunga (long like spaghetti), corta or tagliata (short like penne) or as pastina or minestrina (tiny pieces), further defined by shape (solid or hollow) and surface texture (smooth or ribbed). Since dry pasta keeps for months, it is exported worldwide. Pasta fresca (fresh) is usually made from soft wheat flour and eggs, rolled and shaped by hand or using simple machines, to be cooked within hours or, at most, a couple of days (vacuum packing or freezing prolongs storage). Pasta ripiena applies to filled or stuffed types, such as ravioli and tortellini. Although distribution of fresh pasta is limited, Italians have exported the methods and the experts to make it abroad.

Riso (rice). As Europe's leading rice producer, Italy specializes in varieties of short, ovular grains bred expressly for the extended braising of risotto. Most of the world's rice is the long-grain type suited to boiling or steaming. Rice is grown in much of the Po valley, though the prime risaie lie in Lombardy's Lomellina area, in Piedmont around Vercelli and Novara and in the flatlands between Verona and Mantova in Veneto and Lombardy. Italian rice is grouped in four categories according to size and cooking time, ranging from the small comune or originario to semifino, fino, and superfino. Superfino, due to its tenacity, is suited to classical risotto, though cooking performances vary among a dozen types. Arborio is popular, though chefs often prefer Carnaroli, Baldo or the semifino Vialone Nano.

Salume (salt-cured, air-dried and smoked meat). Most salumi is made from pork in two generic types. The first covers minced meats known as insaccati (encased in protective coverings), such as salame, sausage and mortadella. The second covers whole cuts, such as prosciutto (ham), spalla (shoulder), capocollo (neck), pancetta (belly, sometimes smoked as bacon) and lardo (a solid cut from the back). The salame-sausage category takes in the popular cotechino, soppressata, luganiga and zampone. The whole cut category is led by prosciutto crudo of Parma, also prized from Friuli's San Daniele and other places. The vaunted culatello is a filet of rump aged in lowlands around Parma. Speck is Alto Adige's smoked flank. Sources of salumi range beyond pork to beef (for bresaola), goose, goat, boar, chamois, turkey and more.

Condimenti (condiments, sauces, preserves, seasonings). This field takes in a wide range of preserved foods, such as jams and jellies, dried herbs and spices, canned fruits and vegetables, notably tomatoes, tomato sauce and concentrated paste. Special sauces are the basil-based pesto or the candied fruit and mustard seed mostarda di frutta. Sott'olio (preserved in olive, or other, oil in jars or cans) applies to sun-dried tomatoes, peppers, eggplant, capers, mushrooms, tuna, sardines, anchovies and more. Sottaceti (preserved in vinegar) applies to pickled vegetables and mushrooms. Olives and capers are often preserved in brine. Italy's unique vinegar, Aceto Balsamico Tradizionale, is also classified as a condiment. The traditional type, which has exclusive DOC status in Emilia-Romagna's provinces of Modena and Reggio, is costly because its singular character is developed over at least 12 years of aging in barrels of different sizes and types of wood. Rules specify that the term balsamico applies to the traditional type, but imitation "balsamic vinegar" abounds.

Tartufi (truffles). Among Europe's 30 species of truffles, the most vaunted are the white (or beige to ocher) Tuber magnatum found mainly in Italy. The hills of Piedmont produce the splendidly scented tartufi d'Alba, sniffed out by dogs and dug up by trifolau, who sell them by the gram as one of the world's most expensive foods. Italians eat white truffles fresh, exporting only a precious few during the fall-early winter season. Italy is also a major source of black truffles, preserved and supplied to markets around the world.

Dolci (sweet baked goods, candies, frozen desserts). Not all of the country's dazzling array of desserts is exported, since certain ices, custards and pastries are best fresh. However, Italians abroad are famous for making gelato, cakes and confectionery. Baked goods that are shipped include cakes called panettone, pandoro and colomba, the fruit and nut bread panforte and cookies or biscuits, such as amaretti macaroons, cantucci almond biscuits and savoiardi or ladyfingers. Chocolates take in many types and brands. Other noted confections are torrone (nougat), marrons glacés (candied chestnuts), confetti (sugar-coated almonds) and liquirizia (licorice).

Vino (wine). Italy in most years produces and exports more wine than any other country in the greatest variety of types and styles. Wine is made in all 20 regions, north and south, from an enormous range of native vines and also from international varieties. Italy is renowned for noble red wines for aging, which experts rate among the world's finest, though youthful types of rosso also enjoy success. White wines have improved dramatically in both crisp, light styles and in wood-aged versions of substance and depth. Italy is a major producer of sparkling wines, made by the sealed tank method (as in sweet Asti Spumante) or by bottle fermentation in dry spumanti described as metodo classico.

Most premium wines originate in the more than 350 zones officially classified as DOC or DOCG (for guaranteed). Many typical wines are classified under the category of indicazione geografica tipica or IGT, which often carry the names of regions or provinces. Italy is also the world leader in vermouth, the fortified wine flavored with herbs and spices that originated in Turin.

Caffè (coffee). Italians import beans from the tropics to be roasted, blended and exported (along with the machines) to meet the world demand for espresso, whose rich body and flavor is the result of hotter roasting than for most other coffees. Italy's choice house blends of Arabica and Robusta beans are toasted dark and brittle enough to be pulverized to precise consistency so that steam pressure forces solubles into the cup to give the espresso concentrated texture while emulsifying oils, which heighten aroma and flavor. Espresso machines come with a narrow spigot through which steam is jetted into milk which mounts to a dense froth as it heats for cappuccino. Unless otherwise specified, caffè in Italy means espresso, though that may be distinguished as ristretto or basso (strong), lungo or alto (weaker), or doppio (a double dose). Cooled with ice it's caffè freddo.

Liquori (distilled spirits and liqueurs). The distillate most popular abroad is grappa, made from the pomace of wine, though certain types of brandy, distilled from wine and aged in wood, are also acclaimed. Italy's numerous liqueurs range in flavor from very sweet to very bitter with delightful tones in between. Popular examples are amaretto (with hints of almond flavor and bitter fruits), sambuca (with licorice-like wild elder flowers) and maraschino (with marasca cherries). Bitters may come from blends of distilled spirits with herbs and spices, as well as quinine (as china), green walnuts (as nocino), artichokes or rhubarb. Some of Italy's most famous liquori are sold under individual brands.

DOP, IGP and Organic Foods

Italy has been known for ages for the authentic goodness of produce from gardens and orchards and the unique qualities of foods, such as cheeses and meats, made by artisans following local traditions. A growing number of such foods have been officially protected under European Union regulations approved in 1992.

Two categories were created. The first, known by the initials DOP (for denominazione di origine protetta) applies to "agricultural and food products whose properties are essentially or exclusively derived from their geographical environment, inclusive of natural and human factors, and whose production, transformation and processing are effected in the place of origin. "All phases of production must be carried out within a delimited geographical area."

The second category of IGP (for indicazione geografica protetta) applies to agricultural produce or foodstuffs whose qualities and properties or reputation are derived from their geographical origin and whose production and/or transformation and/or processing occur in the given geographical area. "It is enough that just one phase of production takes place in the designated area."

By 2000, there were 72 DOP and 31 IGP products recognized, though more candidates abound in both categories. The 103 protected foods then included 30 cheeses, 20 types of olive oil, 18 meat-based products and two traditional balsamic vinegars. Yet the foods approved to date represent a fraction of the inventory of local products.

Italy has more culinary specialties than any other country. All of the nation's 20 regions recently presented lists of typical foods, arriving at a nationwide total of 2,171 specialties as candidates for eventual protection. The regional lists take in 376 types of cheeses, plus numerous olive oils, meat products, breads and pastas, as well as vegetables, fruit, grains, legumes, mushrooms and truffles, honey, herbs, spices, condiments and preserves, wine and fruit vinegars, pastries and sweets.

To become eligible for DOP or IGP status, foods must be grown or processed following rules formulated by producers and approved by the European Union. Norms and quality standards are enforced by national commissions. Labels of producers who comply are guaranteed for authenticity throughout the EU, though protected foods are also recognized in other countries.

Italy is the leading European country for organic farming. Some 50,000 farms or estates cultivate nearly 1 million hectares (2,470,000 acres) of land without the use of chemicals and using only organic fertilizers.

Organic farming, which began in the 1960s as an isolated phenomenon, has spread to become a major factor in Italian agriculture. Today there are eight regulatory bodies behind the production of organic produce, which includes fruits and vegetables, olives and olive oil, grapes and wine, grains and animal fodder.

The six southern regions lead the nation in organic farming significantly, accounting for about 75 percent of Italy's organic produce. The warm, sunny southern climates are obviously well suited to natural produce. The islands of Sardinia and Sicily together account for about half of the land devoted to organic farming.

Eating in Italy

Italian meals eaten outside of Italy, however delicious, never taste quite the same as they do at home. It's a question of local produce and the customs of cooking and serving foods peculiar to each place, tied in with a certain atmosphere—the smells and sights and sounds of restaurants, trattorie, taverns, cafés, shops and markets—that can't be duplicated elsewhere.

That might be why visitors come away with fond memories of dining experiences in a country whose social life has always focused on the pleasures of the table. Readers, who still look forward to such pleasures, might find this summary of Italian dining terminology useful.

Pasto is a generic term for meal. Colazione may refer to lunch or a mid-morning repast or, as prima colazione, breakfast, which usually runs to "continental" standards with coffee or tea, bread or pastries and fruit. Merenda, more or less synonymous with spuntino, may refer to a mid-afternoon or mid-morning snack—or light lunch. Cena signifies an evening meal or late supper. Pranzo, which in parts of Italy means lunch (synonymous with colazione) and in other places dinner or supper (synonymous with cena), also refers to an important meal, banquet or business dinner. Local expressions can complicate matters.

Full meals may range through three to six courses (called portate) or sometimes more. Curiously, though, antipasti don't rate a number, even if the range of appetizers offered in some places would constitute a feast. The first course—primo piatto (also simply primo) or minestra—may consist of pasta, risotto, polenta, gnocchi or soup. The second or main course—secondo piatto or piatto di mezzo—may cover seafood, meat, poultry, game, omelets or other cooked cheese or vegetable dishes. The numbering system falls flat when meals include two or more primi or secondi or when a fish entrée, for example, precedes a meat course. With the main course or courses will come a contorno, a side dish or garnish of cooked vegetables, salad, rice, noodles or polenta. Courses may continue with formaggio (cheese), frutta (fresh fruit), dolce (also called dessert), caffè (espresso, of course) and digestivo (grappa, brandy or liqueurs, such as amaro or sambuca).

Terms for public eating places in Italy follow what would appear to be a pattern, but since the categories aren't official, the names can be deceptive.

Ristorante should be a full-fledged restaurant providing complete menus (fixed price or à la carte) cooked by a professional kitchen staff and served by waiters, including a sommelier, experienced with foods and wines. The term, from the French restaurant, came into use after the Risorgimento to describe elegant and sophisticated dining establishments. But, as popularity spread, ristorante also came to apply to pretentious ordinary places.

Trattoria, which suggests familiarity as a derivative of trattare (to deal with or attend to), applies to a neighborhood, small town or rural eating house, often family run, serving local foods and wines. Though the surroundings and service are usually unostentatious, like the price, the classic trattoria should provide exemplary regional cooking. Daily menus are often hand written or chalked on a blackboard or simply recited.

Osteria, from the Latin hospes, originally defined an inn providing food and lodging. But the name came to signify a modest wine house, often serving simple foods—like the similarly cozy taverna or locanda. Such locales have faded. Osteria (or hostaria) suggests simplicity, but the term (like locanda, taverna or trattoria) may apply to a sophisticated eating place.

Pizzeria, the pizza parlor popularized in Naples and the south, provides its specialty baked by a pizzaiolo in a wood-fired oven to be eaten on the premises or taken out. As the most popular type of eatery in Italy, the pizzeria no longer confines choices to pizza, but often provides other dishes, usually at lower prices than a ristorante.

Bar, the English term for a counter or place serving primarily alcoholic beverages, has a broader meaning in Italy, where such establishments abound as gathering places, providing coffee, wine, beer and spirits, soft drinks, pastries, sandwiches, ice cream, candies and more. An "American bar" specializes in cocktails and mixed drinks. The terms snack bar and wine bar often remain in English in Italy.

Caffè originally applied to the coffee house popularized in the 18th century. Although a modern caffè will specialize in espresso-sometimes from its own torrefazione or roasting plant—the term has become synonymous with bar. In Italy, a caffè is not usually a dining place, as a café so often is elsewhere. But there are exceptions.

Birreria was originally a place that served draught beer made in its own brewery, though it now signifies a tavern that specializes in beer but offers other beverages and often a menu with hot and cold dishes.

Terms for shops where food is sold and may be eaten on the premises are rosticceria (specializing in roast meats), tavola calda (hot dishes), tavola fredda (cold foods), paninoteca (sandwiches), gelateria (homemade ice cream). Enoteca (wine library) usually refers to a retail shop, though some enoteche also serve wine and food.

Not all eating and drinking places offer local specialties, since imitation and adoption of foods from other regions is widespread in Italy. You can find spaghetti alla matriciana on menus in Milan and costoletta alla milanese in Rome, peperonata in Verona and polenta in Palermo. You can also find what even Italians call "fast food" just about everywhere.

To taste the foods and wines of Italy at their genuine best, there's no substitute for a visit to their regions of origin. If you do make the trip, buon viaggio and buon appetito!

The South and Islands
Sicily, Sardinia, Calabria, Basilicata, Apulia, Campania

Most of the basic elements - olive oil, wine, cheese, grains, fruits and vegetables - originated in other places, but what came to be known as the Mediterranean diet assumed its enduring character in Italy's south. The Mezzogiorno, as it's often called, was a garden of the Greeks and Romans. The most celebrated foods and wines of the ancient world were produced in these sunny lands at the heart of the Mediterranean.

Yet it isn't historically correct to describe collectively six regions that boast distinct cultural heritages. Two are the Mediterranean's largest islands, Sicily and Sardinia, whose natural isolation explains their idiosyncrasies, but Calabria, Basilicata, Apulia and Campania also follow individual customs. Certain traits can be traced to ancient peoples: the Siculi and Sicani of Sicily, the early Sardinians, the Campani, Apuli, Bruttii, Samnites, Lucani and Messapians of the southern peninsula. Some were colonized by the Greeks of Magna Graecia and all were absorbed into the Roman empire. Southerners shared bonds of unity, if invariably imposed, under Byzantines and Normans and on and off for centuries under French and Spanish rulers of what came to be called the Kingdom of the Two Sicilies. Sardinia, however, often went it's own way, and even today people of the six regions retain their autonomous spirits.

Most outsiders came to conquer, though some introduced concepts of cooking that proved useful (Greeks and Arabs in particular). Yet all eventually surrendered to local tastes, won over by the flavors, aromas and colors of things that grow in the meridional sun.

Olive oil is fundamental, but the symbol of southern cooking, curiously enough, came to be the tomato, which arrived with peppers, beans and potatoes from America. The pomodoro found a promised land alongside the eggplant from Asia, the melanzane that distinguishes the "parmigiana" classics of Campania and many other dishes. The irresistible piquancy of southern food comes from herbs and spices, above all the tangs of garlic and chili peppers.

Italy's first pasta was almost certainly made in the south, though noodles were preceded by flatbreads called focacce, forerunners of pizza, whose spiritual home (if not its place of origin) is Naples. Baked goods, including pastries, biscuits and cakes, abound in the Mezzogiorno, though nowhere as evidently as in Sardinia, where each village has its own styles of bread.

Arabs in Sicily established a pasta industry in the Middle Ages, using durum wheat for the dried types that still prevail in the south. Tubes and other forms of "short" pasta may be referred to generically as maccheroni, distinguished from "long" types such as spaghetti and vermicelli. Also popular are spiral-shaped fusilli, oblique tubes called penne and larger tubes called ziti or zite, though variations make the pasta field as confusing as it is intriguing. Fresh pasta is also prized, sometimes made with eggs but more often not, in such familiar forms as lasagne, fettuccine and ravioli, through there is no shortage of local peculiarities.

Southern geography is marked by often sharp contrasts between

rambling seacoasts and masses of mountains and hills that dominate the interior of most regions. Coastal dwellers have habitually eaten seafood and hill people meat, though preferences aren't always clear-cut. Deep waters of the Tyrrhenian and Ionian seas render tuna and swordfish, shallower waters mollusks and crustaceans for the delectably fresh frutti di mare. Anchovies and sardines are fixtures through the south, though it's also curious to note that all regions have recipes for baccalà or stoccafisso, the dried cod apparently introduced by the Normans.

Historically, meat had been used thriftily in the south, where every part of the animal is still rendered edible. Prime cuts of veal and beef are rare and prized. Lamb and kid are the glories of the hill country, grilled, roasted, braised or stewed in ragouts to be served with pasta. Poultry is popular, as are game birds, boar and hare where available. But the perennial provider has been the pig, preserved in all manner of sausages and salame (often spicy), soppressata, hams, salt pork and lard that in some places substitutes for olive oil in cooking.

Cheese, or cacio, is fundamental in southern diets. Sheep provide pecorino, which may be eaten at early stages of ripeness or aged to be used for grating. Goat's milk is the source of caprino. Ricotta, preferably from sheep, is eaten fresh or used in pasta fillings, pastries and desserts, though it is also salted and dried to be sliced or grated. The most prominent family of southern cheeses are the pasta filata types, which come mainly from cows. The exemplar is mozzarella, originally (and best) from the milk of bufala, water buffalo. The popular cow's milk version is called fior di latte. The oldest member of the clan is caciocavallo, whose name refers to dual forms hanging from strings like saddle bags astride a horse (cavallo). Like the similar provolone, caciocavallo may be eaten after a few months as dolce (mild and tender) or aged for a year or more as piccante (sharp and hard and

suited for grating). Both may be smoked. In between are the spongy provola and scamorza, both eaten young, often cooked or smoked. Burrino is a special pasta filata type with a core of butter.

No other section of Italy boasts such a splendid heritage of sweets and ices. Many desserts bespeak the Greek and Arab influences in Sicily, with its almond pastes, candied fruits, ricotta, honey, raisins and nuts. But anyone with a sweet tooth will find delights all over the south.

Through much of the 20th century, the vineyards of the Mezzogiorno were noted mainly for copious quantities of wine. Apulia and Sicily were perennial leaders in volume, much of it in bulk blending wines shipped to northerly places. But lately producers in all six regions have learned that the future lies in quality. The result has been a rapid improvement in the class and style of bottled wines that increasingly live up to the ancient promise of what the Greeks called Oenotria, the land of wine.

Few places in the Mezzogiorno are known for deluxe restaurants or traditions of haute cuisine. Feasting is reserved for holidays and truly special occasions. The genius of southern cooking lies in the local individuality of everyday fare, the pure and simple preparations of foods whose flavors, aromas and colors capture the essence of the Mediterranean.

22

Sicily (Sicilia)

The culture of fine dining may have been conceived in Sicily when Archestratus, a Greek poet born at Gela in the 4th century B.C., wrote Gastronomia as an ode to the pleasures of the Sicilian table. Outsiders before and since have sung the praises of the bountiful seas and fertile volcanic soils of this island crossroads of the Mediterranean.

The Greeks, among their other contributions to Sicilian cooking, introduced whole grain and refined flours for flatbreads that were forerunners to focaccia. They planted the Malvasia and Moscato vines that are still prominent today. They also seem to have used the snows of Mount Etna to make ices based on fruits and honey.

But the strongest outside influences came from Saracens and other Arabs in the Middle Ages. They brought spices from the east and introduced cane sugar for the making of sorbets, pastries and cakes, including the elaborate cassata that heralded Sicily's reputation as a treasure island of sweets. Arabs founded a pasta industry near Palermo in the 12th century, using grain from fields planted earlier by the Romans. They introduced methods of fishing tuna and swordfish in deep Tyrrhenian waters. Curiously, though, what Sicilians call cùscusu is made with fish, where in North Africa couscous generally contains lamb.

But then, Sicilians have always had a knack for adapting foreign customs to their own uses. Perhaps that's why it's sometimes said that the Siclian way of eating tells more about the original inhabitants, the Siculi and Sicani, than of Greeks, Romans, Arabs, Normans and Aragonese. The modern diet relies on grains, vegetables, herbs and spices, olives and olive oil, fruits, nuts, seafood and cheese. But recipes reveal a miscellany of local tastes

Pasta, usually made from durum wheat semola, takes many forms, ranging from spaghetti and maccheroni (maccaruna in dialect) to zite tubes and gnocchi (or gnocculli). Most celebrated is pasta con le sarde (with sardines and wild fennel, though versions vary from place to place).

Sicily is Italy's second most prominent producer of organic foods after Sardinia. The island's year-round supply of fresh vegetables and herbs triumphs in salads, both raw and cooked. Tomatoes are omnipresent, notably in the southeast around the town of Pachino. Equally adored are eggplants (which may be fried, baked with cheeses or stewed and served cold as caponata) and peppers (which may be grilled, stuffed, baked, or stewed in peperonata).

Palermo is the administrative center of Sicily, whose provinces include Agrigento, Caltanissetta, Catania, Enna, Messina, Ragusa, Siracusa and Trapani. The largest of Italy's 20 regions (25,710 square kilometers), Sicily ranks 4th in population (5,098,000).

Sicilian olive oil is prized, as are the DOP table olives called Nocellara del Belice. The outlying islands specialize in capers, best known as the IGP Capperi di Pantelleria, though the Lipari or Aeolian isles are also noted for these tasty flower buds preserved in sea salt.

Seafood, led by sardines and anchovies that figure in many recipes, is eaten throughout the region. Along the coasts, the features are fresh tuna and swordfish, which may be marinated in oil and herbs, stewed or roasted or cut into steaks and grilled.

Meat is prominent in the central hills, where lamb, kid and pork prevail, though cooks also make good use of veal, poultry and rabbit. Sicilians supposedly invented meatballs, polpetti or polpettoni, which are eaten as a main course with tomato sauce, though abroad they often appear with spaghetti as a caricature of Italo-American cuisine.

Cheeses are dominated by Pecorino Siciliano DOP, also known as tuma or tumazzu, whose pungent flavor is sharpened when laced with peppercorns. When aged and hard, Pecorino is used for grating. Ragusano DOP is a cow's milk cheese, mellow and delicate when young, though it may also be aged hard and sharp for grating. Caciocavallo and provola or provoletta are also popular. Creamy soft ricotta is used in pasta fillings and pastries, though it may also be salted and dried.

The region is a major producer of fruit, notably oranges and lemons, peaches, apricots, figs and table grapes, which rate an IGP from Canicatti. The region is famous for blood oranges, IGP as Arancia Rossa di Sicilia. A delicious curiosity is the prickly pear called fico d'India which grows on cactus.

Sun-dried and candied fruits and nuts go into the dazzling array of sweets. Almonds are the base of marzipan and pasta reale, which is used for the sculpted candies in the form of fruits, a craft begun at Martorana, a monastery near Palermo. The island also produces pistachio nuts, especially prized as a base for ice cream.

Sicily has rapidly taken the lead in winemaking in the modern south, producing an increasing amount of classified wine, including the DOCG red Cerasuolo di Vittoria and 22 DOC appellations. The most renowned DOC is Marsala, once considered the quintessential cooking wine, though in its toasty vergine or solera versions it makes an excellent aperitif and match for ripe cheeses. Sicily is noted for sweet wines, such as Moscato Passito di Pantelleria and Malvasia delle Lipari. But its growing reputation is for dry table wines: rich, complex reds well suited to lamb, pork, poultry and cheeses, and fresh, fruity whites, which go well with seafood and vegetables.

DOP PRODUCTS
Cheeses: Pecorino Siciliano, Ragusano.
Olive oils: Monte Etna, Monti Iblei, Valdemone, Val di Mazara, Valle del Belice, Valli Trapanesi.
Olives: Nocellara del Belice.

IGP PRODUCTS
Produce: Arancia Rossa di Sicilia, Cappero di Pantelleria, Fico d'India dell'Etna, Pomodoro di Pachino, Uva da tavola di Canicatti, Uva da tavola di Mazzarrone.

SPECIALTIES OF SICILY
agghiotta di pesce spada swordfish cooked with tomato, pine nuts, raisins, olives and herbs.
arancini di riso fried rice balls with a core of cheese, peas, chopped meats and tomatoes, which give the "little oranges" their color.
braccioli di pesce spada grilled swordfish fillets wrapped around a cheese-vegetable filling.
cannoli pastry tubes filled with creamy paste of ricotta and candied fruit.
caponata eggplant stewed with tomato, onion, olives and capers

and served as a salad or antipasto. (A seafood version of caponata is rarely seen today).

carciofi ripieni artichokes stuffed with sausage, sardines and cheese and baked.

cassata brick-shaped sponge cake layered and coated with a frosting of ricotta with maraschino liqueur and candied fruit and nuts. Chocolate covered versions and various ice cream or semifreddo cakes are called cassate.

crispeddi or fritteddi fritters of dough flavored with anchovies and wild fennel; crispeddi may also be sweet, made of fried dough or rice sprinkled with sugar and cinnamon.

cùscusu Sicilian couscous based on seafood—dentex, grouper, cod and eel—cooked with tomato and herbs and served on a bed of grainy semolino.

farsumagru large slice of veal or beef, flattened and rolled around a stuffing of chopped ham, sausage, pecorino and eggs and braised in wine with herbs and spices.

fravioli di Carnevale fried sweet ravioli filled with ricotta and cinnamon.

gnocculli semolino gnocchi with ricotta and meat sauce.

melanzane alla siciliana eggplant fried and then baked with mozzarella and tomato sauce.

pasta con la Norma spaghetti with a sauce of eggplant and tomato, favored by Catania's Vincenzo Bellini, who wrote the

opera La Norma.

pasta con le sarde pasta tubes with sauce of fresh sardines, anchovies, onions, raisins, pine nuts, almond, saffron and wild fennel, though ingredients vary.

peperonata bell peppers stewed with onion, tomato and olives, often served cold.

pignolata or pignulata confection of sweet fried dumplings (sometimes chocolate coated) shaped in a mound or cone held together by caramelized sugar with liqueur.

polpettone meatball of ground beef, breadcrumbs, grated cheese and eggs, fried in olive oil and served with tomato sauce.

sarde a beccaficu sardines breaded and stuffed with various ingredients, such as pine nuts and raisins, usually baked but sometimes fried.

scorzette di arance candite candied orange peels.

sfincioni or sfinciuni thick focacce with tomato and cheese, specialty of Palermo; sweet fried rice balls are also called sfuncini.

zite al pomodoro e tonno short pasta tubes with tomato and tuna sauce.

25

Sardinia (Sardegna)

Frequenters of modern Sardinia's beach resorts consider the island a haven for seafood that goes so nicely on summer days with cool white Vermentino or Nuragus. And indeed the rugged coasts provide such delights as rock lobsters, crabs, anchovies, squid, clams and the sardines that may or may not have taken their name from the island. Spicy fish soups are called burrida and cassòla. At Oristano they dry mullet eggs into blocks of delectably pungent bottarga or buttariga to slice thin over pasta or salads.

Yet it's said that the real Sardinian cooking is the rustic fare of the hills and the hearth: roast meats, sausages and salame, savory Pecorino Sardo and Fiore Sardo cheeses and red wines of the weight of Cannonau, Monica and Carignano. Near the town of Nuoro, in the Barbagia hills, they skewer suckling pig called porceddu or lamb or kid on poles of aromatic wood to be turned occasionally as they roast for hours before an open wood fire. Now rare is the method of roasting a carraxiu, in a pit lined with branches of juniper, olive and rosemary, over which is lit a bonfire whose falling embers encase the meat and cook it slowly with the juices sealed inside.

The island bears the marks of outsiders, from Phoenicians, Carthaginians and Romans to Genoese, Pisans and the Savoys who proclaimed the Kingdom of Sardinia. But Spaniards, who ruled for centuries before, lent the most pronounced accents to foods and wines. Still, the cooking of Sardinia remains as wonderfully eccentric as the nuraghe, the prehistoric stone towers whose origins are an enigma.

The sunny island in mid-Mediterranean boasts ideal natural conditions for things that grow, as attested by the fact that Sardinia is Italy's leading producer of organic produce, accounting for nearly a third of the nation's land cultivated by biological methods. Tomatoes are used generously in sauces, as are artichokes, fava beans, peas, eggplant and zucchini. Foods here are redolent of herbs, including wild fennel, juniper and myrtle, used with hare, boar and game birds.

Each Sardinian village bakes its own breads, variations on the large round loaves known as tondus, the doughnut shaped còzzula or stick-like zicchi, though names vary almost as much as do styles. Bakers everywhere share a liking for the flat pane carasau and its crisp variation called carta da musica (music paper). The island boasts a tempting range of sweet biscuits, fritters, pastries and cakes, which often contain almond, ricotta, raisins and elaborate spices.

Cagliari is the administrative center of Sardinia, whose other provinces are Nuoro, Oristano and Sassari. The region ranks 3rd in size (24,090 square kilometers) and 12th in population (1,654,000).

Sardinians consume quantities of dried pasta, in the familiar forms of spaghetti and maccheroni, though they also make the singular ravioli-like culingiones and the gnocchi called is malloreddus, described as the region's most typical dish.

Sardinia, more than any other region, is a land of shepherds, whose Razza Sarda sheep account for the class of Pecorino Sardo and Fiore Sardo DOP cheeses, whether eaten fresh or aged for grating. Sardinia is also a major producer of Pecorino Romano DOP. Also notable are goat's milk cheeses, caciocavallo (or casizolu) and provolone.

Sardinia's classified wines are led by the dry white DOCG Vermentino di Gallura, though the island also boasts 19 DOCs. A lighter version of Vermentino figures among the four regionwide appellations, which also apply to the red Cannonau and Monica and sweet white Moscato. The most distinctively Sardinian of wines is Vernaccia di Oristano, aged in small barrels to take on tones reminiscent of Sherry. Malvasia also shows personality, as do the rare and sweet red Girò and white Nasco from near Cagliari. Lamb and kid are usually served with hearty dry Cannonau (which also makes a Port-like dessert wine), though a sturdy alternative is Carignano del Sulcis. Preferred with fish are the full-flavored Vermentino di Gallura, the bone dry Nuragus di Cagliari and the stylish Torbato under the Alghero DOC.

DOP PRODUCTS
Cheeses: Pecorino Sardo, Fiore Sardo, Pecorino Romano.

IGP PRODUCTS
Meat: Agnello di Sardegna.

SPECIALTIES OF SARDINIA
agnello con finocchietti baby lamb stewed with onion, tomato and wild fennel.

aragosta arrosto rock lobster split in half and pan roasted with olive oil, lemon, parsley and breadcrumbs.

burrida soup or chowder often based on shark meat, though recipes vary from port to port.

cassòla as many as a dozen types of fish, mollusks and crustaceans are cooked with tomato and spices in this piquant soup.

culingiones ravioli with a pecorino-chard filling dressed with tomato sauce, though many variations include a sweet version with almonds.

favata stew of dried fava beans with tomato, cardoons, wild fennel, sausage and salt pork.

fregula or succu tundu lumpy semolino is the base of thick soups that usually include onions, salt pork and grated pecorino.

gallina al mirto boiled hen left to marinate for a day or two with myrtle berries and leaves and eaten cold.

malloreddus tiny gnocchi of semolino (also called maccarones cravaos or ciciones) with sausage and tomato sauce that includes garlic, basil, a hint of saffron and grated pecorino.

pabassìnas pastries topped with a paste of raisins and walnuts; papassinus are similar though the paste also includes aniseed, cloves and cinnamon.

pane fratau carta da musica softened in hot water, spread with tomato sauce topped with grated caciocavallo and a poached egg—a summer dish of the Barbagia.

sa corda or cordula lamb or kid intestines stewed with onion, tomatoes, peas; the meat may also be spit roasted or grilled.

sebadas or seadas sweet focaccia baked with pecorino and bitter honey from blossoms of corbezzolo (the strawberry tree).

su farru soup of farro (barley-like grain) cooked in beef broth with cheese and dried mint.

Calabria

The ancient Greeks lived and dined more lavishly in Calabria than in any other part of Magna Græcia. But the mountainous toe of the Italian boot remained isolated and poor for centuries after, as its cooking took on the tasty integrity of a country tradition.

Calabrians have an appetite for hefty soups and pastas laden with vegetables, headed by eggplants, peppers and tomatoes and ranging on through artichokes, asparagus, potatoes, beans and peas. The red onions of Tropea, a town on the Tyrrhenian coast, are renowned for refined aroma and flavor. The lofty Sila range between Cosenza and Catanzaro abounds in mushrooms, including the prized porcini.

Calabria is a major producer of olive oil, accounting for about 25 percent of the nation's total. The extra virgin oils of Alto Crotonese, Bruzio and Lametia have been singled out for DOP status. Beyond its role in cooking, Calabria's olive oil is used for preserving vegetables, mushrooms and fish.

Alongside the familiar maccheroni and spaghetti, Calabrians make pasta called làgane (similar to fettuccine), ricci di donna (lady's curls), and capieddi 'e prieviti (priest's hairs). Some housewives still make pasta ru ferretto, rolling the dough around slender iron rods to form tubes.

Pork is the region's prevalent meat, preserved as ham, salame and sausages, including the type with bits of liver and lung known as'ndugghia or 'nnuglia (probably from andouille, introduced by the occupying French). Four types of Calabrian salumi qualify for DOP: Capocollo (neck roll), Pancetta (pork belly), Salsiccia (sausage) and Soppressata (a type of salame). Sheep and goats are prized as sources of both meat and cheese. Cows grazed in the Sila range around Cosenza render fine Caciocavallo Silano DOP and butirro, with a core of butter.

The fishing fleet at Bagnara Calabra harpoons swordfish and tuna in Tyrrhenian waters. Anchovies and sardines are also prominent in Calabria, though every town has a recipe for dried cod—baccalà or pesce stocco—often cooked with potatoes, tomatoes and peppers.

Along with ample loaves of country bread, come an array of focaccia and pizza, whether in the Neapolitan style or in local versions: one with ricotta and prosciutto, another with pork crackling and raisins and another called pitta chicculiata.

The region is a major producer of citrus fruit, led by the IGP Clementina di Calabria and the DOP Bergamotto di Reggio Calabria, the bergamot whose oil is used for flavoring and perfumes. A regional

Catanzaro is the administrative center of Calabria, whose other provinces are Cosenza, Crotone, Reggio di Calabria and Vibo Valentia. The region ranks 10th in both size (15,080 square kilometers) and population (2,064,000).

glory is dried figs, either covered or stuffed with chocolate, which is also used to coat lemon and orange peels. Calabrians make a luscious array of pastries and sweets for the Christmas and Easter holidays, though some desserts are available year-round.

Reds dominate the region's 12 DOC wines, led by Cirò, which traces its origins to Magna Græcia. It comes from the Gaglioppo grape, which is also the source of the pale but potent reds of Savuto, Pollino and Verbicaro. Dry whites, led by the crisply fruity Cirò Bianco, generally derive from the Greco grape, as do the exquisitely sweet Greco di Bianco and Greco di Gerace, though they are rarely found away from their sunny vineyards overlooking the Ionian Sea.

DOP PRODUCTS
Cheese: Caciocavallo Silano.
Olive oil: Alto Crotonese, Bruzio, Lametia.
Meat products: Capocollo di Calabria, Pancetta di Calabria, Salsiccia di Calabria, Soppressata di Calabria.
Produce: Bergamotto di Reggio Calabria.

IGP PRODUCTS
Produce: Clementina di Calabria.

SPECIALTIES OF CALABRIA
alalunga in agrodolce tender young tuna cooked in sweet-sour sauce of onion and vinegar.
cannarìculi Christmas fritters made of flour and sweet cooked wine coated with honey.
chinulille sweet ravioli stuffed with chocolate, chestnuts, candied fruit and nougat and fried.
ciambotta stew of eggplant, peppers, potatoes, onions, tomatoes eaten hot or cold.
licurdia onion soup thickened with bread and grated pecorino and laced with hot pepper.
millecosedde vegetable soup whose "thousand things" include cabbage, celery, mushrooms, fava beans, chickpeas and the similar but stronger flavored cicerchie.
murseddu pie of pork and veal liver with tomato and peppers.
mursiellu stew of tripe and pork innards cooked with tomato, peppers and wine.
mùstica baby anchovies preserved in olive oil, also known as "Calabrian caviar."
perciatelli e lumache pasta tubes with snails in a piquant tomato-pepper sauce.
pesce spada alla bagnarese swordfish in the style of Bagnara Calabra, roasted in a casserole with olive oil, lemon, capers and chopped parsley.
pitta chicculiata a type of pizza with tomatoes, tuna, anchovies, black olives and capers.
rigatoni alla pastora pasta tubes with fresh ricotta, sausage and grated pecorino.
sagna chine festive lasagne laden with ground pork, peas, mozzarella, mushrooms, artichokes, sliced hard-boiled eggs and other seasonal ingredients.
sarde a scapece fried sardines rolled in bread crumbs and doused with a mixture of hot oil, vinegar, garlic and mint.

Basilicata

The food of this sparsely populated region may seem as austere as its lonely uplands, yet the cooking emanates a sunny warmth that often becomes fiery, due to the chili pepper called diavolicchio that laces many a dish.

The people of Basilicata—which is also known as Lucania after the ancient Lucani people—share with their southern neighbors a taste for pasta and vegetables, mountain cheeses, lamb, mutton and pork. Since meat had always been used thriftily, the keeping properties of pork were exploited in fine salumi, led by the sausages known as luganiga (from Lucania) and salame or soppressata kept in olive oil or lard.

Minestre cover a range of vegetable and bean soups and pasta in such forms as the hand-rolled tubes called minuich, lasagne with beans and the little dumplings called strangulapreuti (priest stranglers). A substitute for pasta (or risotto) is grano, cooked wheat grains served with a sauce or even as a pudding (as grano dolce). Protected as IGP are beans from the town of Sarconi and bell peppers from Senise.

The region takes pride in its cheeses: pecorino, the goat's milk casiddi and caciocavallo from the ancient Podolica breed of cows. Part of the Caciocavallo Silano DOP is in Basilicata. Cow's milk is also used for manteca, a creamy pasta filata cheese with a filling of butter, and the rare burrino farcito, filled with butter and salame.

Basilicata, though a modest wine producer in terms of volume, boasts a grandiose red in Aglianico del Vulture, which carries the name of a vine introduced by the ancient Greeks and the volcano on whose slopes they planted it. When aged it makes a towering match for lamb and cheeses. Refreshingly tasty are the sweet and often bubbly Moscato and Malvasia.

DOP PRODUCTS
Cheeses: Caciocavallo Silano, Pecorino di Filiano.

IGP PRODUCTS
Produce: Fagiolo di Sarconi, Peperone di Senise.

SPECIALTIES OF BASILICATA
calzone di verdura pizza dough baked folded over a filling of chard, peppers and raisins.
cazmarr stew of lamb's innards, prosciutto, cheese and wine.
ciammotta fried eggplant, peppers and potatoes stewed with tomatoes.

Potenza is the administrative center of Basilicata, whose other province is Matera. The region ranks 14th in size (9,992 square kilometers) and 18th in population (608,000).

31

ciaudedda braised artichokes stuffed with potatoes, onions, fava beans, salt pork.

cotechinata pork rind rolled around a filling of salt pork, garlic and peppers and stewed in tomato sauce.

focaccia a brazzud' flatbread with pork crackling, lard and oregano.

grano al ragù wheat grains boiled and served with a rich ragout made of sausage and salt pork, tomatoes, garlic, olive oil and white wine and topped with grated pecorino.

grano dolce pudding of wheat grains, blended with chocolate, walnuts, pomegranate seeds and vin cotto (sweet "cooked wine").

peperonata con carne di porco pepper and tomato stew with various pieces of pork.

pignata di pecora ewe cooked with potatoes, tomatoes, onions, pork and pecorino in a clay pot called a pignata.

pollo alla potentina chicken braised in wine with onion, tomato, peppers and basil.

scarcedda Easter tart with ricotta and hard-boiled eggs.

spezzatino di agnello lamb stewed in an earthenware pot with potatoes, onions, bay leaf and peppers.

torta di latticini cheesecake based on ricotta, mozzarella and pecorino with pieces of prosciutto.

zuppa di pesce alla Santavenere soup based on grouper, scorpion fish and other Ionian seafood with plenty of garlic and pepper.

Apulia (Puglia)

This long, slender region whose tip, the Salento peninsula, forms the heel of the Italian boot, consists of rolling plains and gentle uplands, ample sources of wine, olive oil and grain. Apulia has been known for abundance since Phoenicians and Greeks arrived and found Oscans and Messapians—some of whom lived in trulli, dwellings with conical stone roofs—were already competent farmers. Although the Apulian diet draws its sustenance from the land, fish from the Adriatic and Ionian Seas lends an enviable balance.

Vegetables figure prominently in pastas, soups, stews and salads. Apulia is the domain of the fava (the "queen of beans"), though artichokes, chicory, turnip greens, the "rocket" green called ruca or rucola, cabbage, cauliflower, eggplant and peppers are indispensable. A curiosity are lampasciuoli, onion-like bulbs of notable nutritive value, whose bitterness brings a unique tang to Apulian dishes.

Pasta, from the region's supplies of durum wheat, range through variations on maccheroni, spaghetti and lasagne to the small shells called orecchiette (or strascinati) and cavatieddi, served mainly with vegetables or tomato sauces, usually with garlic and peppers. Rice is also esteemed, notably in tiella, which refers to an earthenware baking dish, though the name may have derived from the Spanish rice dish of paella. Tortiera is a casserole, whose various ingredients are gratinéed with pecorino or caciocavallo or pane grattugiato, breadcrumbs, which substitute for cheese in many southern dishes.

The Adriatic and Ionian seas provide a wealth of seafood and frutti di mare. Especially prized are oysters and mussels from beds in the Gulf of Taranto, though the range includes octopus, cuttlefish, squid, anchovies, sardines and sea urchins.

The Murge plateau provides grazing land for lamb and kid, the preferred meats, though the diet is enhanced by beef and poultry and pork as the base of an ample array of salumi. Cheeses cover the southern gamut of pecorino and pasta filata varieties, though among the latter burrata (whose name refers to the buttery softness of its cream-filled interior) stands out from the towns of Andria and Martina Franca.

Bread from the town of Altamura has been recognized as DOP. Apulian bakers also specialize in the flat focaccia (or puddica) and variations of pizza from both wheat flour and potatoes. These include calzoni, calzuncieddi, panzerotti and sfogliate, in which the dough is

Bari is the administrative center of Apulia, whose other provinces are Brindisi, Foggia, Lecce and Taranto. The region ranks 7th in both size (19,357 square kilometers) and population (4,032,000).

folded over a filling and fried or baked. Biscuits are also popular, especially the doughnut shaped frisedde and the curly taralli. A rich array of pastries and sweets is enhanced by such ingredients as ricotta, almonds for marzipan, candied fruit and honey.

As a prolific grape producer, Apulia had been a perennial source of potent red wines shipped north for blending. But lately the quality side of production has come to the fore, represented by 25 DOCs, the most of any southern region. Notable among them are the crisp whites of Locorotondo and Martina Franca, the reds and rosés of Castel del Monte and the Salento peninsula, where such appellations as Salice Salentino, Brindisi, Copertino and Alezio have been gaining admirers outside the region.

DOP PRODUCTS
Cheeses: Canestrato Pugliese, Caciocavallo Silano.
Olive oils: Collina di Brindisi, Dauno, Terra di Otranto, Terre di Bari, Terre Tarentine.
Olives: La Bella della Daunia.
Bread: Pane di Altamura.

IGP PRODUCTS
Produce: Clementine del Golfo di Taranto.

SPECIALTIES OF APULIA
agnello al cartoccio lamb chops baked in paper or foil with lampasciuoli and olives.
bocconotti half-moon shaped pastry shells flavored with Marsala and filled with cream and jam and baked.
carteddate ribbons of pastry dough flavored with Marsala rolled and fried in olive oil and topped with honey and cinnamon; purciduzzi are similar.
cavatieddi con la ruca pasta shells with cooked rocket greens, tomato and pecorino.
ciceri e tria chick peas and noodle soup.

cozze alla leccese mussels baked with oil, lemon and parsley.
frisedde biscuits softened with water and served with olive oil, tomato and oregano.
gniumerieddi skewers of lamb or kid innards with slices of salt pork, pecorino and bay leaves grilled over the coals of a wood fire.
melanzane alla campagnola eggplant sliced, grilled and served with olive oil, chopped garlic, basil and mint.
melanzane ripiene baked eggplant hollowed and stuffed with its chopped pulp, tomatoes, breadcrumbs, capers, olives, anchovies.
'ncapriata thick soup of fava beans mashed with bitter chicory.
orata alla barese gilt-head bream roasted with potatoes, garlic, grated pecorino.
orecchiette con cime di rapa ear-shaped pasta shells with turnip greens, garlic, chili peppers.
ostriche alla tarantina Taranto oysters breaded and baked with olive oil and parsley.
seppie ripiene small cuttlefish baked with a stuffing of chopped mussels and squid, capers, breadcrumbs, grated pecorino.
tiella di cozze mussels baked with rice, potatoes, tomatoes, onions, grated pecorino.
zuppa alla tarantina peppery soup of shellfish with grouper, eel, prawns and cuttlefish simmered with tomatoes and served with toasted garlic bread.

Campania

The ancient Romans, who dubbed it Campania Felix, marveled at the fertility of its volcanic soils. So did the Greeks who founded Neapolis on the gulf bounded by Mount Vesuvius, Pompeii, Sorrento and the islands of Capri and Ischia. Naples, under the royal houses of Anjou and Bourbon, long reigned as a capital of haute cuisine. Yet, almost in spite of the noble resources of sea and countryside, the city became a sanctuary of street food.

The prima donna of the byways is pizza napoletana, in authentic versions known as marinara (with tomato, garlic and oil) and Margherita (with tomato, mozzarella and basil). Ingredients are rigorously selected by pizzaioli, who work the dough with a master touch so that when baked in a matter of moments in a searing hot wood-fired oven the crust puffs to a bread-like softness with a delectable hint of crunch.

There are, of course, many types of pizza baked in Naples, as well as calzoni (pizza dough folded over a filling) and focaccie of all description. Street foods extend through a range of fried, grilled, sautéed, baked and frozen delights sold at shops and kiosks and from carts that ply the narrow streets and alleyways. The fact that they may be eaten standing up doesn't detract at all from their inherent goodness.

Neapolitans are also devoted to pasta: maccheroni, spaghetti, vermicelli, fusilli, perciatelli and ziti, among others. The pasta sauce of predilection is pummarola from the rare, tiny plum-shaped San Marzano tomatoes that are protected by DOP in the Sarnese-Nocerino area in the fertile valley to the southeast of Vesuvius in the provinces of Avellino and Salerno.

Campanians have been known as mangiafoglie (leaf eaters) because greens and vegetables so dominated the diet. In the sun-drenched fields around Vesuvius and the gulf, eggplants, tomatoes, zucchini, various types of peppers, salad greens, garlic and herbs reach heights of flavor, as do peaches, apricots, figs, grapes, melons, oranges and lemons.

The large, thick-skinned lemons of Sorrento and the Amalfi coast are renowned as the source of the liqueur called limoncello. Chestnuts and hazelnuts from the hills of Avellino enjoy IGP status. Olive oils from the Cilento and Sorrentine peninsulas and the hills of Salerno enjoy DOP status.

Naples (Napoli) is the administrative center of Campania, whose other provinces are Avellino, Benevento, Caserta and Salerno. The region ranks 12th in size (13,595 square kilometers) and 2nd in population (5,793,000).

Seafood is a mainstay of the Neapolitan diet, especially the compact creatures that go so well in antipasto and pasta or deep fried in a grand fritto di pesce. The gulf abounds in little clams called vongole veraci, mussels, tender young octopus, cuttlefish, squid, prawns, shrimp, anchovies and the smelt called cecenielli.

City dwellers have never been avid meat eaters; some smother steaks in tomato sauce alla pizzaiola. But country people in the hills around Benevento and Avellino prefer lamb and pork, veal, poultry and rabbit. Campania's hill people also make fine salame and prosciutto, along with tangy pecorino cheese.

Water buffalo grazed in marshy lowlands around Capua and Salerno yield the ultimate in mozzarella di bufala—too fine in its pristine state, admirers insist, to melt onto pizza when cow's milk fiore di latte will do. They prefer it within hours of when its strands are pulled like taffy and formed into rounds like snowballs that do indeed melt in the mouth. The DOP of Mozzarella di Bufala Campana differentiate the cheese from widespread imitations.

Ricotta and mascarpone from buffalo are also prized, as are provola and scamorza, which are sometimes lightly smoked. A specialty of Sorrento are caprignetti alle erbe, golf ball-sized goat's milk cheeses rolled in herbs. Caciocavallo and provolone are popular. Part of the Caciocavallo Silano DOP is in Campania. The prized grating cheese is Parmigiano-Reggiano®, protagonist in dishes called parmigiana with eggplants, zucchini and other vegetables.

Naples is justly proud of its pastries and sweets, among which sfogliatelle ricce, pastiera, struffoli and zeppole are legendary. Gelato is often made from fresh fruit and nuts. Icy granita is usually flavored with lemon or coffee. Some say the secret of Napoli's seductively sweet espresso is a pinch of chocolate in the coffee grounds.

The grandest cru of ancient Rome was Falernum, whose vineyards

lie in northern Campania. Today, Falerno, as one of the region's 19 DOCs, is respected in its red and white versions, as are wines from around the Gulf of Naples that carry the names of Ischia, Capri and Vesuvius (as Lacrima Christi del Vesuvio). But the most vaunted wines of Campania come from the heights to the east in the Irpinia hills in the province of Avellino: the red Taurasi and the white Greco di Tufo and Fiano di Avellino, all of which rank as DOCG.

DOP PRODUCTS
Cheeses: Mozzarella di Bufala Campana, Caciocavallo Silano.
Olive oils: Cilento, Colline Salernitane, Penisola Sorrentina.
Produce: Pomodoro San Marzano dell'Agro Sarnese-Nocerino.

IGP PRODUCTS
Meat product: Vitellone Bianco dell'Appennino Centrale.
Produce: Carciofo di Paestum, Castagna di Montella, Limone Costa d'Amalfi, Limone di Sorrento, Nocciola di Giffoni.

Specialties of Campania
baccalà alla napoletana salt cod with tomato, black olives, raisins, pine nuts, capers, garlic.
cianfotta peppers, eggplants, zucchini, onions and basil stewed in olive oil and served cold.
coniglio all'ischitana rabbit braised with tomatoes, rosemary, basil and white wine Ischia style.
coviglie al caffè coffee mousse topped with toasted beans and whipped cream; coviglie al cioccolato is the chocolate version served with a candied cherry.
mozzarella in carrozza the cheese (sometimes with filet of anchovy) is pressed between slices of white bread, coated with batter and deep-fried.
'mpepata di cozze mussels cooked in their juice with lemon, parsley and black pepper.
parmigiana di melanzane eggplant fried and then baked with onions, tomato, basil, mozzarella, topped with grated Parmigiano-Reggiano®.
pastiera napoletana Easter pie with a filling based on ricotta flavored with candied fruit, lemon and cinnamon.
peperoni imbottiti red and yellow bell peppers stuffed with anchovies, black olives, capers, garlic, breadcrumbs.
polpi affogati baby octopus "drowned" in boiling salt water, then sautéed with olive oil, tomatoes and hot peppers.
ragù napoletano this festive ragout of beef (or pork) braised to tenderness in an earthenware pot with onions, tomatoes, basil, olive oil and red wine is often served with maccheroni.
sartù an extravagant mold of rice with beef, chicken livers, sausage, peas, mushrooms, tomato, mozzarella and more; the name comes from surtout, as it was described by French aristocrats.
sfogliatelle ricce curly pastry shells with a sweet filling of ricotta, candied fruit and spices.
spaghetti alla puttanesca "strumpet's style" with tomato sauce, black olives, capers, anchovies, garlic, chili pepper-specialty of Ischia.
struffoli sweet fried dumplings massed into a cone held together with honey and flavored with candied fruit.
taralli ring-shaped biscuits baked with almonds and lard, or sometimes fennel seeds; the sweet types with vanilla, cinnamon and liqueur are called tarallucci dolci.
zeppole di San Giuseppe puffy pastry fritters sometimes with a creamy filling.
ziti ripieni large pasta tubes stuffed with chopped pork and salame, onion, raw eggs and caciocavallo cheese.
zuppa di cozze mussels in a soup of tomatoes, white wine, parsley and hot peppers.

39

Central Italy
Molise, Abruzzi, Latium, Umbria, Tuscany, Marches

Art and literature have emphasized the extravagant banquets of Renaissance courts, the revelry of Medieval hunting and harvest feasts, the conspicuous consumption of ancient Romans. Yet, barring the occasional episodes of excess, patterns of eating in central Italy have historically upheld the culture of country cooking and the virtues of simplicity and balance.

The diet in all six regions adheres to Mediterranean standards in its reliance on olive oil, grains and seasonal produce. But cooking styles vary markedly in a territory split into ethnic enclaves by the Apennines, the mountainous spine of the peninsula. In ancient times, the Adriatic side was inhabited by Sabellian and Oscan tribes of the Abruzzi and Molise and Piceni and Senone Gauls of the Marches. On the Tyrrhenian side, Latium was inhabited by Latins and Sabines, Umbria by Umbri, while Etruscans from their base in Tuscany gained territory up and down the peninsula before being subdued by the Romans.

Notions of unity were advanced under the Roman Empire, but for centuries after its fall the various states of central Italy struggled to assert autonomy against the menace of foreign invaders and the hegemony of papal Rome. Umbria and the Marches remained largely loyal to the papacy. The Abruzzi, of which Molise was a province until 1963, maintained historical ties to southern regimes. Tuscany, despite battles between Florence and other city states and long periods of foreign rule, upheld a measure of independence.

Historical patterns still reflect in regional diets. As the national capital, Rome serves as an intermediary between north and south in political as well as culinary matters. Abruzzi and Molise show a southern touch in dishes that are decisively piquant. The Marches shares recipes with central neighbors as well as Emilia-Romagna to the north. Tuscany and Umbria have tastes in common, though throughout the heartland cooks uphold traditions in local ways.

The ancient grain called farro (spelt) is still used in soups. Until recent times, the chestnut was the leading staple of the diet in the uplands of the Apennines. Eaten roasted or boiled, chestnuts were also dried and ground into flour for polenta, soups, flat breads, cakes and pastries. They were even used to fatten pigs. Today, of course, wheat is the base of pasta and most bread, including the unsalted loaves unique to Tuscany, Umbria and the Marches.

Overall the use of pasta is about evenly split between dried and fresh types in the central regions, where rice and polenta play secondary roles. Abruzzi and Molise have solid traditions of

40

maccheroni. In Latium, spaghetti, bucatini and rigatoni share the spotlight with Rome's egg-based fettuccine. Dried pasta is produced in quantity in Umbria and the Marches, though cooks still often hand roll the dough for tagliatelle and local delights. Homemade noodles are also preferred in Tuscany, but that's one place where bread historically outweighed pasta.

Fine olive oil is made through the central hills, where the paragon of extra vergine comes from hand-picked olives. Garden produce is rigorously seasonal. Rome is renowned for artichokes and peas, Tuscany for white beans and black cabbage, the uplands of Abruzzi, Umbria and the Marches for lentils, chickpeas and potatoes. The central Apennines are a major source of truffles, both the prized white varieties found in the Marches and parts of Tuscany and the black varieties that thrive in Umbria.

Consumption of fresh seafood was historically confined to coastal areas. Each Adriatic port boasts a proud recipe for the fish soup called brodetto. Along the Tuscan coast the counterpart is cacciucco. But even in inland places, such as landlocked Umbria, cooks made good use of preserved anchovies, tuna, sardines and salt cod.

Meat plays a key role in regional diets, with preferences for lamb and kid to the south and veal and beef to the north, particularly in Tuscany whose Chianina steers provide the legendary bistecca alla fiorentina. Poultry and rabbit are appreciated everywhere, as are game birds, hare and wild boar in regions where hunting is still considered more a birthright than a sport.

Pork is prominent everywhere, in the salumi made by butchers whose ancient craft was perfected in the Umbrian town of Norcia. The Marches, Latium, Umbria and Tuscany all claim the origins of porchetta, a whole pig boned and stuffed with garlic, wild fennel, rock salt and peppercorns and roasted slowly in wood-burning ovens.

Pecorino is the dominant cheese in all regions, though styles range from soft, young marzolino (made from milk of sheep or goats grazed on green grass in early spring) to firm and tangy types to aged Pecorino Romano, hard and sharp and used mainly for grating.

The so-called renaissance in Italian wine gained impetus in Tuscany, renowned not only for the classics of Chianti, Brunello di Montalcino and Vino Nobile di Montepulciano but also for individualistic reds often called "Super Tuscans." The red Montepulciano of the Abruzzi has won growing acclaim, as has the Sagrantino of Umbria. But some of the best known wines of central Italy are white: the Marches with Verdicchio, Umbria with Orvieto and Latium with Frascati and other wines of the Castelli Romani.

41

Molise

This small, sparsely populated region shares a gastronomic bond with Abruzzi, its historical partner to the north, though the proximity of Apulia and Campania lend its foods a southern accent. It's also nice to know that Molise in its unassuming way harbors culinary secrets of its own.

The region is noted for robust fare of authentically rustic goodness, specialties of the towns and villages that grace the hillsides from the short strip of Adriatic coast to the rugged heights of the Apennines, home of the ancient Samnite tribes.

In the hills, lamb, kid and mutton are popular, along with pork for sausages, salame and soppressata, sometimes preserved in terra-cotta vases under fine local olive oil. Prosciutto may be salt cured, though it is also smoked—rare in Italy. Prominent cheeses are caciocavallo from the town of Agnone, pecorino and scamorza. The port of Termoli provides triglie di scoglio (red mullet, base of a tasty soup), fresh anchovies, squid, crabs, clams and sea snails.

Molise produces quantities of dried pasta, though in country homes women still often roll the dough by hand. Specialties include sagne (lasagne), laganelle (tagliatelle), crejoli (similar to the Abruzzi's maccheroni alla chitarra) and recchietelle (orecchiette). Pasta is often served with ragout of lamb and pork, invariably with diavolillo (chili pepper), and a grating of sharply flavored pecorino cheese. The tomato, fresh or preserved, is omnipresent in Molise, as are beans and artichokes. Campobasso is noted for giant white celery.

Polenta is as popular as pasta in places. Cornmeal is cooked in a mush, though the flour may also be used for a type of pizza. Molise has a tasty array of cakes, biscuits and pastries, and one of the most bizarre of desserts: blood sausage with chocolate and pine nuts.

Most of the region's limited sources of wine are consumed locally. The three DOCs—Biferno, Molise and Pentro di Isernia—cover reds, whites and rosés, some of which have gained a reputation beyond the region.

DOP PRODUCTS
Cheese: Caciocavallo Silano.
Oil: Molise.
Meat product: Salamini Italiani alla Cacciatora.

Campobasso is the administrative center of Molise, whose other province is Isernia. The region ranks 19th in both size (4,438 square kilometers) and population (334,000).

42

IGP PRODUCTS
Meat product: Vitellone Bianco dell'Appennino Centrale.

SPECIALTIES OF MOLISE

abbuoti or torcinelli involtini (envelopes) of lamb intestines filled with chopped liver, sweetbreads, hardboiled egg and baked.

baccalà alla cantalupese salt cod cooked with peppers, capers, black olives, grapes, garlic.

calcioni di ricotta rustici rounds of pasta dough filled with ricotta, provolone and prosciutto fried in olive oil—often part of a fritto misto.

lepre a ciffe e ciaffe hare cooked in a marinade of vinegar and wine with plenty of herbs.

panettoncino di mais spongy corn-flour cake with chocolate.

pezzata ewe stewed with tomato, onion, rosemary and hot peppers.

picellati pastries filled with honey, nuts and grapes.

pizza con le foglie corn flour flatbread baked with wild greens; pizza e minestra is a soup of pork broth and field greens with the pizza crumbled into it.

polenta maritata slices of cornmeal fried in oil with garlic and layered with a filling of red beans and peperoncini and baked in the oven—specialty of Isernia.

zuppa di ortiche soup of early spring nettle sprouts cooked with tomato and bacon.

43

Abruzzi (Abruzzo)

The people of this mountainous Adriatic region are known as hearty eaters. The maximum expression of gourmandise was la panarda, a meal of 30 to 40 courses eaten through a day—an extravaganza no longer in vogue. Today's menus are robust and often pungent but rarely complex. The Abruzzi is renowned for its chefs, though many have made their reputations abroad.

The Adriatic provides shellfish, anchovies, mullet, octopus, cuttlefish and the varied makings of brodetto (a peppery soup for which each port has its own version). Streams and lakes provide trout, eels and crayfish. Yet what seems to be a healthy majority of Abruzzesi look to the land for nourishment.

The basic elements are olive oil, tomatoes and the chili pepper called diavolicchio (among other local terms), which is used as generously here as anywhere in the south. The uplands around the highest peaks of the Apennines produce outstanding artichokes, cardoons, beans, lentils and potatoes and the nation's main supply of saffron, the thread-like orange-red stigmas of the crocus flower used as an exotic spice. Saffron, under the DOP of Zafferano dell'Aquila, may be the most costly of foods, far passing truffles or caviar in value per gram.

Abruzzi is renowned for dried pasta, exemplified by maccheroni alla chitarra (quadrangular strands formed by the strings of what resembles a guitar). In country kitchens, heaps of pasta or polenta were spread on the spianatora, a large board at center table from which each guest helped himself. Abruzzesi are also fond of soups from vegetables and beans or with the crepes called scrippelle in broth.

Lamb and kid are preferred meats--grilled, roasted or braised in ragouts served with pasta or polenta. Pork products include the fine salame called mortadellina from the town of Campotosto, ventricina (peppery sausages usually spread on bread) and salsicce di fegato pazzo ("crazy liver" sausages sweetened with honey and spices). Pecorino and caciocavallo are key cheeses, though local delights are the goat's milk capruzzo, often preserved in olive oil, and scamorza, from cows grazed on high plateaux, tasty fresh or grilled.

Alongside an array of fine pastries, biscuits and cakes, the Abruzzi produces confetti, sugar coated almonds given out at

L'Aquila is the administrative center of Abruzzi, whose other provinces are Chieti, Pescara and Teramo. The region ranks 13th in size (10,794 square kilometers) and 14th in population (1,250,000).

weddings and other celebrations, and torrone, nougat here often coated with chocolate.

The region has only three DOCs, so they are easy to remember. Montepulciano d'Abruzzo, a full-bodied red wine which rates as DOCG in the Colline Teramane zone and DOC elsewhere, also covers a cherry pink Cerasuolo, a robust rosé. The red, which is attractively supple when young, can also age impressively. The youthful white Trebbiano d'Abruzzo DOC goes well with fish, though in rare cases it can age to mellow grace. Controguerra DOC applies to various types of wine, red and white. Mountain herbs are used in Abruzzi to make liqueurs, the best known of which is Centerbe, drunk as a digestivo.

DOP PRODUCTS
Olive oils: Aprutino Pescarese, Colline Teatine, Pretuziano Colline Teramane.
Meat product: Salamini Italiani alla Cacciatora.
Produce: Zafferano dell'Aquila.

IGP PRODUCTS
Meat product: Vitellone Bianco dell'Appennino Centrale.

SPECIALTIES OF THE ABRUZZI
agnello alle olive lamb cooked in an earthenware pot with olive oil, black olives, lemon, oregano, hot peppers.
cicoria, cacio e uova soup of wild chicory and other vegetables with salt pork in chicken broth thickened with eggs and grated pecorino.
coda di rospo alla cacciatora monkfish cooked with garlic, rosemary, anchovies, peppers.
lasagne abruzzese pasta sheets with a peppery meat and tomato sauce.
maccheroni alla chitarra noodles often served with a ragout of lamb stewed in wine and olive oil with tomatoes, garlic, bay leaf and peppers.
mazzarelle d'agnello lamb's lung and innards wrapped in beet greens or chard and braised in white wine.
'ndocca 'ndocca pungent stew of pork ribs, feet, ears and skin with rosemary, bay leaf, peppers and vinegar.
pizza rustica pork sausage, mozzarella, eggs and Parmesan baked in a pie.
polpi in purgatorio octopus cooked with tomato, garlic, parsley and diavolicchio.
scapece di vasto pieces of raw fish-such as ray and smooth hound shark-preserved in earthenware vases with salt, chili peppers and saffron.
scrippelle 'mbusse or 'nfuss fried crepes (or dumplings) coated with pecorino and served in chicken broth.
timballo di crespelle crepes layered with spinach, artichokes, ground meat, chicken giblets, mozzarella and grated Parmesan baked in an elaborate mold.
virtù soup of Teramo that according to legend was made by seven damsels who contributed various ingredients, including pieces of pork, beans, peas, greens, herbs, carrots, garlic, onions, tomato and pasta.
zuppa di cardi soup of giant cardoons from L'Aquila with tomatoes and salt pork.
zuppa di lenticchie e castagne tiny mountain lentils and fresh chestnuts in a soup with tomatoes, salt pork and herbs.

45

Latium (Lazio)

The Eternal City has been a melting pot for foods from other places since the Roman legions began collecting recipes and provisions—and, in some cases, cooks—from the far reaches of the empire. As the national capital, Rome has drawn culinary inspiration from Italian regions north and south, though most substantially from the home provinces of Latium.

Today, in a world center of art, religion and trade, Roman eateries cater to visitors ranging from diplomats and jet-setters to pilgrims and backpackers. This compulsory cosmopolitanism may explain why precious little has been preserved of the epicurism of the ancient Romans or of the papal and princely courts of later eras. Yet what remains of la cucina romana provides some of the most flavorful foods of Italy served in some of its liveliest surroundings. For, beyond the gastronomic aspects, eating is a social event to Romans, who love to gather family and friends around tables as plates, glasses and bottles multiply with the passing hours.

Memorable meals begin with arrays of antipasti that alone would make feasts: platters of frutti di mare, anchovies, sardines, tuna, fried shrimp, prosciutto, salame, olives, mushrooms, pickles, sun-dried tomatoes, sweet-sour onions, peas and beans with pork, pizze, focacce, canapés, vegetable tarts, frittate with potatoes and onions, stuffed eggplants, peppers and tomatoes, croquettes of rice, vegetables or meats, breads grilled and flavored with garlic and oil as bruschetta or sliced and topped with meat and vegetable pastes or cheeses as crostini.

Latium's gardeners, who raise the tastiest of peas, zucchini and fava beans, specialize in artichokes tender enough to eat raw—or to cook in the style of Rome's Jewish ghetto as carciofi alla giudia. The region's own species of rucola (rocket) and the wild ruchetta make splendid salads, as do puntarelle, spear-like endive dressed with raw garlic and anchovies.

Roman menus feature spaghetti alla carbonara and bucatini all'amatriciana, as well as tubes of rigatoni and penne. Fresh pasta may be flat as lasagne, rolled as cannelloni or cut in strips as the celebrated fettuccine al burro—often identified with a restaurant called Alfredo. Gnocchi from potatoes or semolino are also popular around the region, as are polenta and rice.

Seafood plays a largely utilitarian role in the daily diet, with mussels, clams, shrimp, squid, cuttlefish and palombo shark fresh from the ports of Fiumicino and Anzio, alongside the indispensable baccalà. But

47

Rome (Roma), the national capital, is also the administrative center of Latium, whose other provinces are Frosinone, Latina, Rieti and Viterbo. Latium ranks 9th among the regions in size (17,227 square kilometers) and 3rd in population (5,140,000).

restaurants cater to expensive tastes with large prawns called mazzancolle and gamberi, sea bass called spigola, as well as imported oysters and lobsters.

Romans adore abbacchio, milk-fed lamb roasted for Easter feasts though delicious year-round. They also eat their share of beef and veal, whose prime cuts were traditionally reserved for the bourgeoisie and whose other parts—tripe, brains, entrails, liver, heart, even feet and tails—went into the zestful dishes of the common people. Pork is prized as porchetta, roasted by butchers in the Castelli Romani and sliced warm for sandwiches at the city's street markets. Many recipes rely on guanciale, salt pork from the jowl, though the traditional lard has been steadily replaced as a cooking fat by olive oil from the Sabine hills.

Pecorino Romano prevails among cheeses, though Latium also makes fine mozzarella di bufala, the similar provatura and tasty young marzolino from the milk of sheep or goats. Ricotta may be eaten fresh or salted and dried for grating.

Rome is noted for gelato, Lenten raisin buns called maritozzi, cream-filled pastries called bignè, rum-soaked fruit and nut cake called pan giallo and a custard cake drenched with syrupy liqueurs known as zuppa inglese (though it's neither soup nor English). The city's coffee bars are famous for espresso from freshly roasted beans. Meals often end with a glass of sweet sambuca liqueur, sipped with three coffee beans to munch on.

Latium is intrinsically linked to white wine—to Frascati and Marino and the other golden-hued bianchi of the Castelli Romani, as well as to the fabled Est! Est!! Est!!! from the northern Latium town of Montefiascone. Yet some of the finest wines are the reds of Cerveteri, Velletri and a trio of DOCs from the Cesanese vine grown in the Ciociaria hills.

48

DOP PRODUCTS
Cheeses: Mozzarella di Bufala Campana (provinces of Latina and Frosinone), Pecorino Romano, Ricotta Romana.
Olive oils: Canino, Sabina.
Meat products: Salamini Italiani alla Cacciatora

IGP PRODUCTS
Bread: Pane Casareccio di Genzano.
Meat products: Mortadella Bologna, Vitellone Bianco dell'Appennino Centrale.
Produce: Carciofo Romanesco del Lazio, Kiwi di Latina.

SPECIALTIES OF LATIUM
abbacchio alla cacciatora baby lamb cooked with rosemary, garlic, anchovies, vinegar.
baccalà in guazzetto salt cod in a sauce of olive oil, onions, tomato, pine nuts, raisins.
bucatini all'amatriciana slender pasta tubes with salt pork, chili pepper and grated pecorino--some include tomato and garlic in the sauce.
carciofi alla giudia tender artichokes flattened flower-like and deep fried; carciofi alla romana are sautéed in olive oil with garlic and mint.
coda alla vaccinara oxtail stewed with onion, tomato, lots of celery and white wine.
coratelle con carciofi lamb or kid liver, heart and lungs braised in olive oil and white wine with hearts of artichoke.
cozze alla marinara mussels steamed in their juice with garlic, tomato, parsley.
fagioli con le cotiche stewed white beans with pork rind, prosciutto, onion, garlic, rosemary.
fettuccine al burro feather-light egg noodles with butter, cream and grated Parmesan.
involtini alla romana veal rolls with chopped guanciale and garlic braised with tomatoes.
mazzancolle alla griglia large prawns grilled with a brushing

of olive oil and lemon

pasta e ceci soup of chickpeas with garlic, rosemary and pasta noodles.

penne all'arrabbiata pasta tubes with a "raging" sauce of tomatoes, garlic and chili pepper.

pollo alla romana young chicken braised in olive oil and white wine with green peppers, tomatoes and garlic

pomodori ripieni large tomatoes hollowed and baked with a filling of their pulp, rice, potatoes, garlic and basil--usually served cold as antipasto.

rigatoni con la pajata squat pasta tubes with sauce based on beef intestine cooked with tomato, salt pork, garlic, herbs and spices, topped with grated pecorino.

saltimbocca alla romana veal fillets with prosciutto and sage sautéed in butter and white wine.

spaghetti alla carbonara guanciale sautéed in oil with garlic and chili peppers is mixed in a bowl with raw eggs, which curdle as they stick to the hot spaghetti--topped with grated pecorino and Parmesan.

spaghetti all'aglio, olio, peperoncino chopped garlic, chili pepper and parsley heated in extra virgin olive oil flavor the al dente spaghetti as it finishes cooking in the pan.

stracciatella lightly beaten raw eggs form stracce (ragged strips) when stirred into hot beef broth flavored with nutmeg and topped with grated Parmesan.

supplì al telefono fried rice balls whose core of mozzarella stretches like telephone wires when divided; sometimes the filling includes bits of veal, liver or anchovy.

49

Umbria

This compact region at the core of the peninsula is known as the green heart of Italy. Its attractions include the art and architecture of its hill towns—Perugia, Assisi, Orvieto, Spoleto and Todi, among them—and the legends of its many saints, led by Francis of Assisi. But connoisseurs also know that nowhere in Italy are the pleasures of country cooking and local wines offered more graciously than in Umbria.

Since the region has no access to the sea, its peoples—beginning with the ancient Umbri and Etruscans, who inhabited territories on opposite sides of the Tiber River—have always relied on the generosity of the land. There are few secrets to Umbrian cooking, other than the native's insistence—or obsession, really—on home-grown produce: fresh vegetables and fruit, dense green olive oil, roast meats, poultry and game, pecorino cheese and the herbs, greens and mushrooms that grow spontaneously on wooded hillsides.

Add truffles and even the humblest dish becomes divine. Norcia, a town on the edge of the Apennines, is Italy's prime source of black truffles, served fresh with pasta, meat and egg dishes, or even pounded into paste with anchovies and garlic. The "black diamonds" are preserved in various ways, including in cheese known as pecorino tartufato. Even more prized are Umbria's white truffles, always eaten fresh.

Norcia is also the ancestral home of pork butchers, noted for salumi that range beyond prosciutto and salame to such specialties as mazzafegati (piquant liver sausages with orange rinds, pine nuts and raisins). Porchetta is delicious in Umbria, as are Perugia's Chianina beef, lamb, rabbit, free-range chickens and wood pigeons. Hare and boar are prized, as are fish and eels from Lake Trasimeno and the upper reaches of the Tiber.

Umbria produces a large share of dried pasta for the national market, though its homemade egg pasta, notably tagliatelle with ragout, can rival the elite of Emilia. Other hand-rolled types are ciriole and stringozzi, which resemble rustic spaghetti.

The Umbrian diet relies on salads and cooked vegetables, notably cardoons (called gobbi) and lentils from the mountain town of Castelluccio. In the autumn, woods abound with porcini mushrooms and chestnuts. Olives grown in the Nera valley near Spoleto and around Lake Trasimeno produce some of Italy's finest extra virgin oil.

Perugia is the administrative center of Umbria, whose other province is Terni. The region ranks 16th in size (8,456 square kilometers) and 17th in population (817,000).

Huge loaves of unsalted pane casereccio are baked in wood ovens, as are torte—spongy flour and egg breads flavored with pecorino or pork crackling. Bakers also make sweet buns called pan nociato (with walnuts, grapes, cloves and pecorino) and pan pepato (with almonds, walnuts, hazelnuts, raisins and candied fruit) and cakes called ciaramicola and torcolo.

Umbria's best known wine is the white Orvieto, historically sweet or abboccato, but now usually dry. Less renowned but even more coveted by cognoscenti are two reds—the venerable Torgiano riserva and the voluptuous Sagrantino di Montefalco—both of which rank as DOCG.

DOP PRODUCTS
Cheese: Pecorino Toscano.
Meat products: Prosciutto di Norcia, Salamini Italiani alla Cacciatora.
Olive oil: Umbria.

IGP PRODUCTS
Meat products: Prosciutto di Norcia, Vitellone Bianco dell'Appennino Centrale.
Produce: Lenticchia di Castelluccio di Norcia.

SPECIALTIES OF UMBRIA
agnello arrosto baby lamb with rosemary, sage, garlic and oil cooked to tender perfection in a covered roasting pan amid the dying embers after bread is baked in a wood oven.

anguille alle brace freshwater eels marinated in white wine, pepper, bay leaf and grilled.
ciaramicola eggs, lard, lemon rind and Alchermes (a spicy liqueur) go into this circular cake topped with candy-specked meringue.
cipollata onion soup with tomato, salt pork, basil and grated Parmesan.
gobbi alla perugina deep fried cardoons topped with meat and tomato sauce.
lepre alla cacciatora hare braised in red wine with sage, bay leaf and garlic.
fave con le cotiche thick soup of fava beans with rosemary and pork rind.
palombacci alla ghiotta spit-roasted wood pigeons with an elaborate sauce of wine, lemon, vinegar, sage, garlic, rosemary, juniper berries and chicken livers.
spaghetti alla nursina black truffles heated in olive oil with a hint of garlic and anchovy flavor this special pasta from Norcia.
stringozzi al pomodoro handmade noodles with tomatoes, black olives and garlic.
tegamaccio stew of freshwater fish—pike, carp, tench, eel—with garlic and peppers.
torcolo sponge cake with raisins and candied fruit, specialty of Perugia.

51

Tuscany (Toscana)

Florentines like to relate how their Caterina de' Medici, on marrying King Henry II in 1533, introduced the recipes and cooks that ennobled French cuisine. It's true that in Renaissance Florence gastronomy reached peaks of refinement among the aristocracy, yet what has distinguished Tuscan food since the time of the Etruscans has been its noble simplicity.

Country cooking attests to the seasonal goodness of garden produce and the perennial splendor of green-gold extra virgin olive oil. Tuscans are fanatical about freshness: fava beans, artichokes and asparagus in the spring; tomatoes, cucumbers and zucchini in the summer; all sorts of greens and mushrooms (especially plump porcini) in the fall; cabbages and chard in the winter. The region is a major source of white truffles, notably from the hills around San Miniato and San Giovanni d'Asso. Herbs, above all rosemary and sage, are good year-round, as are the fresh or dried white beans—toscanelli, cannellini, zolfini—the fagioli that earned them the epithet of mangiafagioli.

Bread is the pillar of the diet, giant loaves of saltless pane toscano redolent of sourdough and wood smoke. Thick slices are grilled, rubbed with garlic and doused with oil as fettunta or panunto. When firm, the bread is dampened and crumbled into a salad with tomatoes, onion and basil as panzanella or spread with chicken liver pâté or chopped tomatoes as crostini. It thickens soups called ribollita, pappa al pomodoro or simply zuppa di pane.

In Tuscany pasta had been historically upstaged by soups, whether or not they included bread. But pasta is by no means ignored. No country feast would be complete without tagliatelle con ragù. Also invariably homemade are the wide-ribbon pappardelle, served with hare or duck sauce, and pici, rustic hand-rolled spaghetti. Rice and polenta also play roles in the diet.

Tuscany was a major producer of saffron in the Middle Ages, notably at the hill town of San Gimignano, where it has recently been revived as Zafferano di San Gimignano DOP. Growingly prized is farro, the ancient grain, predecessor of wheat, that is used whole in soups or ground into flour as a base for pasta and breads.

Seafood prevails along the coast, where Livorno's cacciucco is a piquant soup. Salt cod and tripe bring zest to the diet, though Tuscan cooking is rarely highly spiced and never boringly bland. That's

53

Florence (Firenze) is the administrative center of Tuscany, whose other provinces are Arezzo, Grosseto, Livorno, Lucca, Massa-Carrara, Pisa, Pistoia, Prato and Siena. The region ranks 5th in size (22,992 square kilometers) and 9th in population (3,577,000).

because food is intended to go with wine, above all the red Chianti, Brunello di Montalcino and Vino Nobile di Montepulciano that are known as vini da arrosto.

The glory of Tuscan meats is bistecca alla fiorentina, a hefty slab of Chianina beef, seared over hot coals so that the juicy red interior is enclosed in a charred crust. Arrosto misto is a platter of roast meats that might include pork, pigeon, rabbit, duck, free-range chicken, thrush, pheasant and guinea hen. Wild boar, a source of salami, sausage and prosciutto, may be stewed with sweet-sour sauce.

Pork is popular as grilled ribs (rostinciana), roast loin (arista), spit-roasted livers wrapped in bay leaves (fegatelli) or porchetta. It is also used for sausages, prosciutto and salame known as finocchiona (flavored with wild fennel seeds). A legend among Tuscan salumi is lardo, a fat cut of pork from the lower back, aged with salt, herbs and spices in marble coffers at the village of Colonnata, where it is known as Lardo di Colonnata IGP.

Pecorino is most savory from sheep grazed on moors near Siena. Mild young, when it may be called marzolino, it is eaten in the spring with raw fava beans. When aged in small wheels coated with olive oil, ash or tomato, it becomes firm with a distinctly elegant tang. Bakers, beyond their daily loaves, also make flatbread called schiacciata, sometimes with rosemary or in a sweet version with grapes. Most Tuscan sweets are baked. Almonds flavor Prato's crunchy biscottini or cantucci and the soft ricciarelli of Siena, a town more renowned for its chewy fruit and nut cake called panforte. Anise flavors wafers called brigidini and a raisin cake called buccellato. Fruit jams are used in tarts called crostate. Florence's pride is zuccotto, a dome-shaped sponge cake flavored with chocolate, nuts and liqueurs.

Chestnuts were a staple of the hill country diet for centuries. The prized type known as marrone is often roasted over wood colas. Dried chestnuts are the base of flour known as Farina di Neccio in the Garfagnana hills, where it rates a DOP. The flour is used in castagnaccio, a flat cake with pine nuts and rosemary, and crepes called necci. Tuscany is also a major producer of honey, classified as Miele della Lunigiana DOP in the northwestern corner of the region.

Chianti in its eight zones is the archetypal Tuscan wine, though DOCG has also been granted to Brunello di Montalcino, Vino Nobile di Montepulciano, the red of Carmignano and the white Vernaccia di San Gimignano. The field of DOCs has grown to cover most of the region, including the coast where the Bolgheri DOC includes a special niche for Sassicaia, a Cabernet that led the aristocratic array of individualistic wines called "Super Tuscans." Meals often end with Vin Santo, aged in barrels to an amber hue with flavor that ranges from lusciously sweet to dry and toasty.

DOP PRODUCTS
Cheeses: Pecorino Toscano, Pecorino Romano.
Honey: Miele della Lunigiana.
Meat products: Prosciutto Toscano, Salamini Italiani alla Cacciatora.
Olive oils: Chianti Classico, Lucca, Terre di Siena.
Produce: Farina di Neccio della Garfagnana, Zafferano di San Gimignano.

IGP PRODUCTS
Meat products: Lardo di Colonnata, Mortadella Bologna, Vitellone Bianco dell'Appennino Centrale.
Olive oil: Toscano.
Produce: Castagna del Monte Amiata, Fagiolo di Sorana, Farro della Garfagnana, Fungo di Borgotaro, Marrone del Mugello,

SPECIALTIES OF TUSCANY
acquacotta "cooked water," soup of vegetables and herbs, often

salt pork, mushrooms and other ingredients, depending on the season.

arista di maiale pork loin roasted with rosemary, garlic and wild fennel seeds.

baccalà alla fiorentina salt cod fried and then stewed with tomatoes, onions, garlic.

cacciucco alla livornese chowder of various fish, including mollusks and crustaceans, with tomato, garlic, onion, carrots, celery, wine, hot peppers, though individual versions abound.

cibreo classic Florentine chicken stew of giblets, embryonic eggs and cockscombs.

cinghiale in dolceforte wild boar stewed with red wine and herbs, augmented at the end with sweet-sour sauce of vinegar, sugar, nuts, raisins, candied fruit and bitter chocolate.

fagioli al fiasco white beans stewed with olive oil, sage and garlic in a thick glass wine flask set amid wood coals.

garmugia or gramugia soup of fava beans, artichokes, peas and asparagus, an ancient recipe of Lucca.

minestra di farro thick soup of farro with onion, tomato, celery and grated pecorino.

pappa col pomodoro tomato, garlic and basil simmered with broth and thickened with bread that melds into a tasty pap.

pappardelle alla lepre wide ribbon noodles with sauce of hare braised with wine, carrots, celery, onions.

ribollita dense soup of white beans with carrots, onions, tomato, black cabbage (though recipes vary) "reboiled" with bread and served with a dousing of olive oil.

trippa alla fiorentina tripe with tomatoes, broth, wine, herbs and grated Parmesan—served on a slice of bread at Florence's markets as lampredotto.

55

Marches (Marche)

In this gentle hilly region between the Adriatic and the Apennines, cooks draw from sea and land and with enviable ease bring the best of both to the table. Fish prevails in the port of Ancona, whose brodetto calls for exactly 13 types in a spicy broth with garlic and tomato. The Adriatic provides the freshest of seafood—sardines, hake, bream, sole, red mullet, crustaceans and mollusks—but Ancona is also famous for the dried cod called stoccafisso or stocco.

The Marches fits central Italian stereotypes with its fine olive oil and pecorino, as well as unsalted bread. But it also feels the culinary influence of Emilia-Romagna with its fresh egg pasta and salumi. Around Pesaro and Urbino, they vary Romagna's cheese-based passatelli by adding meat to the mixture. Macerata is the home of vincisgrassi, a legendary lasagne crowned—in season—with white truffles, which flourish in the Marches.

Menus cover a thorough mix of meats: quail, pigeon, guinea fowl, chicken, rabbit, lamb, beef and pork. It's curious to note that seafood and meat may be cooked in similar ways. For example, poultry, fresh fish or even dried cod are often done in potacchio (with onion, tomato, white wine and rosemary), while duck, rabbit, ham or even sea snails may be done in porchetta (with wild fennel, garlic and rosemary).

The region that stakes persuasive claims to the origins of porchetta, also makes an impressive range of salumi. Notable are the prosciutto of Montefeltro, specifically from the town of Carpegna, the salame of Fabriano and the cotechino of San Leo. Around Macerata they make a sort of sausage called ciauscolo, soft enough to spread on bread like pâté.

At Ascoli Piceno, giant olives are stuffed with a meat-cheese-bread filling and deepfried. Zucchine and peas are favored in season, while beans and chickpeas are used year-round for soups. Greens include ròscani, whose spinach like leaves have an acidic bite.

Pecorino is preferred young and mild, sometimes almost sweet. The rare ambra cheese from the town of Talamello is a formaggio di fossa made from a mix of sheep and cow's milk into forms wrapped in cloth and buried in pits carved out of tufa where mold forms during fermentation and accounts for uniquely sharp flavor.

Cheese often figures in focaccia and pizza, as well as in desserts, which are usually moderately sweet. Ravioli-like pastries are Ascoli's calcioni (made with fresh pecorino) and Macerata's piconi (with

Ancona is the administrative center of the Marches, whose other provinces are Ascoli Piceno, Macerata and Pesaro-Urbino. The region ranks 15th in size (9,693 square kilometers) and 13th in population (1,426,000)

ricotta, rum and cinnamon). Corn flour is used in Ancona's beccute (biscuits with raisins and nuts) and frustenga (cake with figs, raisins and walnuts).

The region's wines are led by Verdicchio, a white that goes well with fish, though it sometimes has the weight to accompany poultry, veal and rabbit. Ancona's pride is the DOCG Conero, a full-bodied red from the Montepulciano grape. Rosso Piceno, from vineyards to the south, can also show class. Vernaccia di Serrapetrona DOCG is a curiosity as a sparkling red wine. Meals in the Marches often end with Mistrà, an anise liqueur traditionally drunk in the coffee cup with the remains of an espresso.

DOP PRODUCTS
Cheese: Casciotta d'Urbino.
Meat products: Prosciutto di Carpegna, Salamini Italiani alla Cacciatora.
Olive oil: Cartoceto.

IGP PRODUCTS
Meat product: Mortadella Bologna, Vitellone Bianco dell'Appennino Centrale.
Produce: Lenticchia di Castelluccio di Norcia.

SPECIALTIES OF THE MARCHES

anatra in porchetta roast duck stuffed with wild fennel, salt pork, garlic.
minestra di ceci soup of chickpeas with pork ribs, tomato, herbs and grated pecorino served over slices of toasted bread.
muscioli arrosto mussels, their shells filled with ham, breadcrumbs and parsley, roasted in tomato sauce.
passatelli di carne ground beef and bone marrow, spinach, cheese, breadcrumbs and eggs worked into paste and forced through slots to form noodles, served like pasta or cooked in broth as soup.
pollo in potacchio spring chicken braised with onion, tomato, white wine, rosemary.
quaglie in tegame quails braised in a pot with white wine, salt pork, tomatoes, peas.
ravioli ai filetti di sogliola pasta envelopes with a ricotta-parsley filling dressed with a sauce of sole with white wine and tomatoes.
stocco all'anconetana dried cod or stockfish cooked with olive oil, white wine, milk, tomatoes, carrots, garlic, rosemary.
vincisgrassi lasagne layered with a sauce of chicken giblets, mushrooms, veal brains and sweetbreads, ham, béchamel, Parmesan and, in season, truffles—preferably white.
zucchine ripiene small zucchini marrows hollowed and stuffed with ground veal, tomato, onion, parsley and grated Parmesan and fried.

Northern Italy
Emilia-Romagna, Liguria, Lombardy, Piedmont, Valle d'Aosta, Veneto, Friuli-Venezia Giulia, Trentino-Alto Adige

The eight regions of what is loosely defined as northern Italy boast the nation's highest standard of living and its richest diet, in terms of both abundance and variety. The plains that extend along the Po and lesser rivers from Piedmont to the northern rim of the Adriatic proliferate with grain, corn, rice, fruit, livestock and dairy products. Vineyards on slopes along the great arc formed by the Alps and Apennines are Italy's prime sources of premium wine.

Restaurateurs and recipe collectors abroad acclaim the common heritage of what they call "northern Italian cuisine." But menus that mix Bologna's tagliatelle and ragout, for example, with Genoa's trenette noodles and pesto, Milan's risotto and braised veal shanks, Venice's black rice and soft shell crabs, Trieste's goulash and sauerkraut or Turin's cheese fondue and white truffles mock historical realities. Even today, despite standardization of tastes and the invasion of fast food, no other section of Italy maintains such diversity in regional cooking.

Roots of local cultures can be traced to early peoples: the Liguri of the Riviera, the Salassi and Taurani of Piedmont, the Rhaetians of the Alpine rim from Lombardy to Friuli, the Veneti of the northern Adriatic basin and the Etruscans who crossed the Apennines to control the Padana valley before the conquests of Cisalpine Gauls and Romans. The unity constructed under the Roman empire collapsed in the Middle Ages. The northern states, domineered by foreign forces, continued to switch loyalties, leaders and borders with dizzying frequency through the Renaissance and on up to the Risorgimento.

The assortment of local dialects, or in some cases full-fledged languages (French in Valle d'Aosta, German in Alto Adige), attests to the historical heterogeneity of Italy's north. French influences remain in recipes of Piedmont, Liguria, Lombardy and Emilia to the northwest, just as Austro-Hungarian tangs linger in foods of the Tre Venezie (Veneto, Friuli-Venezia Giulia and Trentino-Alto Adige) to the northeast. But local tastes rule in this vast territory where culinary customs vary delectably from province to province and town to town.

Still, some generalizations might be made about northern cooking. Meat has prevailed over seafood in most places where butter and lard are the traditional fats. Exceptions must be made for Liguria, with its exemplary Mediterranean diet, and the Adriatic strip where seafood and olive oil prevail. In most inland areas, diets have relied on a wholesome mix of grains, legumes, cheeses, preserved fish and seasonal varieties of vegetables, mushrooms and herbs. A tendency to substitute olive oil for animal fats has revitalized the balance.

Pasta, rice, polenta and gnocchi figure in one form or another in each region's diet, though local preferences present a study in contrasts. Fresh pasta, usually made with eggs, prevails south of the Po in Piedmont, Liguria and, most gloriously, in Emilia-Romagna. Rice dominates in the flatlands of Lombardy and Piedmont, where it is usually braised and stirred as risotto, and in the Veneto, where it is often simmered in broth in dishes that range tastily between risottos and thick soups.

59

Polenta, made from corn or also from buckwheat or chestnut flour, was the sustenance of northern country people for ages, eaten as a mush or porridge with cheese or sauces or sliced and fried or grilled to go with meat dishes. Today's polenta strongholds are the Tre Venezie and the Alpine flanks of Lombardy and Piedmont. Gnocchi are often based on potatoes, though dumplings are also made from semolino or ricotta and greens. In Trentino-Alto Adige, round bread dumplings are called Knödeln or canederli.

Perhaps the most popular category of primi—though not only a first course—are soups, which may include pasta, rice, polenta, gnocchi, bread, vegetables, beans, meats or seafood. Prominent examples of northern minestre are the noodle and bean pasta e fagioli of the Veneto and Friuli, the fish chowders of Liguria and the Adriatic coast, Milan's tripe-based busecca and Emilia-Romagna's delicate pasta in brodo (afloat in broth).

A meat dish eaten nearly everywhere in the north is bollito misto. But the mix varies between beef, veal, pork sausages and poultry, while sauces range from parsley-based salsa verde to Piedmont's tomato red bagnet ross, Verona's beef marrow and pepper pearà and Cremona's candied fruit and mustard mostarda. Fritto misto is also eaten in most regions, though compositions of fried meats, cheeses, vegetables, fruits and pastries are never the same from one place to another.

Pork plays a prime role in salt-cured meats, whose hallmark is Prosciutto from Parma and San Daniele, the salt-cured ham described as dolce due to the ripe flavor and soft texture that develop over a year or more of maturing. But the delights of salumi range beyond pork to beef for the bresaola of Lombardy's Valtellina, as well as goat, goose and chamois for salame and sausages.

Northern Italy is a paradise for cheese lovers. They may begin with Parmigiano-Reggiano® and Grana Padano, which account for a major share of national production, and nibble their way through blue-veined Gorgonzola, buttery Fontina, tangy Asiago and a vast array of mild, creamy, ripe and sharp cheeses, mainly from cows but also from sheep and goats.

The eight northern regions produce about a third of Italian wine, though they account for more than half of the DOC/DOCG total. The leading region for volume of classified wines is Veneto, where Verona's Soave and Valpolicella head production. Trentino-Alto Adige and Friuli-Venezia Giulia have sterling reputations for white wines, though they are increasingly admired for reds. Lombardy is noted for aged reds from the Alpine Valtellina and classical sparkling wines from the hills of Franciacorta and Oltrepò Pavese. The north's most vaunted reds are Barolo and Barbaresco of Piedmont, a region that also makes Gattinara, Barbera, Dolcetto and sparkling sweet Asti.

A byproduct of wine is grappa, which was long considered a common sort of spirit. But class has been upgraded dramatically in recent times by distillers in Friuli, Veneto, Trentino and Piedmont, whose grappa often comes from select grape varieties and specific vineyards.

Emilia-Romagna

As Italy's capital of gastronomy, Bologna was known as la grassa (the fat), a description less flattering today than it once was. But the city still gloats over a land of plenty that extends along the fertile southern flank of the Po. Emilia (to the west of Bologna) and Romagna (to the east) flaunt their considerable differences, but together share Italy's most luxuriant tables.

Recipes, like the names of dishes, vary from town to town in a region that breeds culinary heroes: Ferrara's Cristoforo di Messisbugo, who chronicled the lavish menus of Renaissance courts; Parma's Duchess Marie Louise (wife of Napoleon), whose tastes inspired generations of dishes; Modena's Este dukes, who fostered the cult of aceto balsamico, the monarch of vinegars; Forlimpopoli's Pellegrino Artusi, the author known as the father of modern Italian cooking.

The honor roll of foods is led by pasta—made with fresh eggs and rolled by hand by a sfoglina to achieve perfect texture. The universal primo is tagliatelle con ragù, though cooks consider the meat sauce personal works of art. Bologna, whose specialties include green lasagne and curly gramigna, disputes with Modena the creation of tortellini (modeled after Venus's navel). Parma's prides are large square envelopes called tortelli and the rounded anolini, which are also made in Piacenza, home of the bean-shaped pisarei. Ferrara's cappellacci (big hats) are stuffed with squash. Reggio's cappelletti (little hats) differ from pasta of that name in Romagna, whose specialties include the rolled tubes called garganelli and slim dumplings called passatelli. Pasticcio is pasta with other ingredients baked in a pie, though interpretations vary.

Polenta, once a staple of the country diet, now plays a secondary role to pasta in the region, as do rice and gnocchi. Vegetables, greens and legumes of all sorts are grown here, though they are often cooked in soups or with pasta. Green asparagus has an IGP from the town of Altedo. Romagna has a native species of shallot protected as IGP Scalogno di Romagna. Mushrooms from the Apennines are prized, notably from around Borgotaro, where they enjoy IGP status. Romagna produces olive oil, protected under DOP for Colline di Romagna and the town of Brisighella.

Baked nearly everywhere are hard wheat rolls of snow-white interiors and tawny crusts called coppiette, due to their shape resembling a "coupled" set of horns—and protected as IGP under Pane

Bologna is the administrative center of Emilia-Romagna, whose other provinces are Ferrara, Forlì, Modena, Parma, Piacenza, Ravenna, Rimini and Reggio nell'Emilia. The region ranks 6th in size (22,124 square kilometers) and 8th in population (3,960,000).

Coppia Ferrarese. Local versions of flatbreads abound. Most renowned is Romagna's circular piadina or piada, baked on tiles (or griddles) and folded over prosciutto, cheese or greens. Thicker focaccia is called spianata or torta salata, though with salt pork in the dough it becomes crescentina at Bologna. In Emilia's hills, paper-thin borlengo or burleng is cooked like a crêpe, dressed with salt pork, garlic and rosemary, folded into quarters and served with grated Parmigiano. Similar flavorings are used on the muffin-like tigelle, baked between tile disks.

Crisp fritters are made throughout Emilia, originally fried in lard but now more often in oil, sometimes flavored with pork crackling, prosciutto or sausage, though types vary. Examples are burtleina at Piacenza, torta fritta at Parma, gnocco fritto at Modena, chizza at Reggio. Bologna's renowned fritto misto combines pastry fritters with fried meats and vegetables. The filling of fried cassoni includes spinach and raisins.

In Emilia, the curing of pork is an age-old master craft. Prosciutto di Parma, Italy's best known meat product, is protected by DOP, as is the rare but even more prized Culatello di Zibello, a filet of rump aged in the foggy lowlands along the Po. Bologna is noted for giant loaves called Mortadella, though the IGP extends through the region and beyond. Modena pig's foot sausage zampone is eaten nationwide at the New Year with lentils for luck. DOP protects Zampone Modena and Prosciutto Modena, while IGP applies to Cotechino Modena, a sausage whose stuffing includes bits of rind.

Piacenza is a center of salume production, with DOP applied to Coppa Piacentina, the neck roll, elsewhere called capocollo, as well as Salame Piacentino and the un-smoked bacon known as Pancetta Piacentina. Ferrara's salama da sugo blends choice bits of pork in a juicy stuffing with red wine, cinnamon, cloves and nutmeg. Emilians all make lean and mildly seasoned salame gentile.

The Romagnola breed of cattle is covered by the IGP of Vitellone Bianco dell'Appennino Centrale. Other meats appreciated throughout the region are veal, turkey, capon, chicken and rabbit. Romagnuols have a taste for duck and grilled and roast pork, lamb and mutton. Cesenatico is the seafood haven of Romagna, whose brodetto is among the tastiest of the Adriatic's fish soups. Eels from the Comacchio lagoon may be stewed, roasted or grilled.

Emilia's Parmigiano-Reggiano®, the "king of cheeses," is firm yet brittle enough to break into bite-sized chunks of elegantly mellow flavor. Aging makes Parmigiano golden and hard for grating. The similar Grana Padano is also made in the region. Romagna's formaggio di fossa was originally produced at Sogliano al Rubicone. Made from a mix of sheep and cow's milk, forms are wrapped in cloth and ripened in underground pits for months to develop rich, sharp flavor. Ravaggiolo and squaquarone are tangy cream cheeses often used in cooking.

Sweets seem almost sinful after such rich fare. That may explain why fruit, especially home grown peaches, cherries, strawberries, pears and cantaloupe, as well as nuts, are prominent in the diet. Of special note are the cherries of Vignola and the pears, peaches and nectarines protected as IGP in Romagna. Chestnuts thrive in the Apennines, where the Marrone del Castel Rio rates an IGP.

Emilia-Romagna boasts its share of biscuits, pastries, tarts, sweet ravioli and tortelli, sherbets and ices. Traditional desserts include Bologna's certosino (spice cake), Ferrara's torta di mele (apple cake), Modena's bensone (lemon-flavored crumble), Romagna's gialletti (cornmeal biscuits) and piada dei morti (flatbread with nuts and raisins).

Aceto balsamico tradizionale is aged at least 12 years in barrels of different types of wood to become dark, dense and almost too divine to be called vinegar. The traditional type is protected by a DOP in Modena and Reggio, but imitations abound. The tradizionale is a unique condiment for meat, fish, and vegetables or the prime ingredient in sauces. Vinegars of 20 years old or more may be sipped from a teaspoon as a cordial or digestive.

Emilia-Romagna is major producer of wine, ranking fourth in volume among the regions. The region has 20 DOC zones and a lone DOCG in the white Albana di Romagna, historically sweet but today mainly dry. In Emilia, where most wines are bubbly, the perfect foil for luxury fare is vivacious red Lambrusco—dry, however, not sweet. In Romagna, hearty red Sangiovese goes with meats and cheeses and the dry white Trebbiano is preferred with fish. Emilia's preferred digestivo is nocino, a liqueur made of green walnuts steeped in distilled spirits.

DOP PRODUCTS

Cheeses: Grana Padano, Parmigiano-Reggiano®, Provolone Valpadana.

Meat products: Coppa Piacentina, Culatello di Zibello, Pancetta Piacentina, Prosciutto di Modena, Prosciutto di Parma, Salame Piacentino, Salamini Italiani alla Cacciatora.

Olive oils: Brisighella, Colline di Romagna.

Vinegars: Aceto Balsamico Tradizionale di Modena, Aceto Balsamico Tradizionale di Reggio Emilia.

IGP PRODUCTS

Bread: Pane Coppia Ferrarese.

Meat products: Cotechino Modena, Mortadella Bologna, Zampone Modena and Vitellone Bianco dell'Appennino Centrale.

Produce: Asparago Verde di Altedo, Fungo di Borgotaro, Marrone di Castel Rio, Pera dell'Emilia-Romagna, Pesca e Nettarina di Romagna, Scalogno di Romagna.

SPECIALTIES OF EMILIA-ROMAGNA

anguilla alla comacchiese eel from the Comacchio cooked in a tomato-onion-garlic sauce.

anolini alla parmigiana a stracotto of various meats, vegetables and herbs makes a filling for the envelopes cooked and served in capon's broth with a liberal grating of Parmigiano-Reggiano®.

asparagi alla parmigiana green asparagus served with melted butter and grated Parmigiano-Reggiano®.

cappelletti romagnoli the "hats" with a filling of cheese, pork, turkey breast, sage and rosemary are served with a pork ragout or in broth.

cappone ripieno large capon roast in the oven with a stuffing of veal, ham and Marsala.

erbazzone round tart baked or fried with spinach or chard, salt pork, onions, garlic, sometimes ricotta, typical of Reggio—called scarpazzone when baked in a crust.

garganelli pasta tubes with ragù alla romagnola based on chicken livers, veal, prosciutto, tomatoes, herbs and béchamel

gramigna short, curly pasta tubes often served with sausage braised in wine.

lasagne verdi Bologna's spinach green pasta sheets layered with ragout and béchamel.

passatelli grated grana, breadcrumbs, eggs and bone marrow are worked into paste and forced through slots to form dumplings, cooked in beef broth as soup in Romagna.

pasticcio di tortellini in Bologna, the cooked pasta with ragù is baked in a pie crust with broth, grated cheese, breadcrumbs and, when available, white truffles.

pisarei e fasò tiny pasta rounds with reddish borlotti beans, tomato sauce and grated Parmigiano-Reggiano® -the pride of Piacenza.

prosciutto con melone roseate slices of Parma ham with fresh cantaloupe (or figs).

riso con sugo di anatra selvatica risotto of the lowlands around Ravenna and Ferrara with a sauce from wild duck stewed with white wine, tomato and herbs.

tagliatelle alla duchessa chicken livers browned in butter flavor noodles dressed with beaten egg yolks and grated Parmigiano-Reggiano®, as Parma's Marie Louise liked them.

tortelli con le erbette envelopes filled with ricotta and greens are served with drawn butter around Parma.

tortellini in brodo the pasta curls with an exquisite meat and cheese filling are traditionally served in capon broth with grated Parmigiano-Reggiano®.

Liguria

The Mediterranean diet takes on touches of genius along the Italian Riviera, which extends from the central port of Genoa in narrow strips to the east (Levante) and west (Ponente). Ligurian cooks rely on the sea, yet their skills shine with produce from the steep hillsides: pale golden olive oil, garden greens, meats and poultry, mushrooms, nuts, herbs, the ingredients for the sauces they call tocchi (touches), above all basil and garlic for the glorious green pesto.

Ligurians, whose ancestors once dominated northwestern Italy and southeastern France, were noted as seafaring traders long before their famous son Christopher Columbus opened channels for foods from America. Pasta tubes called macheronis were cooked in the 13th century by Genoese, who spread the cult of noodles to other Italian ports and over the Apennines to Emilia. Ancient Ligurians made polenta and breads from the flour of dried chickpeas and chestnuts. It's been speculated that a form of pasta originated there as the lasagnette strips of chestnut flour that still appear on menus.

Liguria remains an active producer of pasta, though these days mainly the dry type based on durum wheat. Preferred with pesto are slender trenette noodles or the short, spiraled trofie or troffiette. The sauce was made by pounding fresh basil in mortar and pestle with garlic and pine nuts (or walnuts), then blending in olive oil and grated Pecorino Sardo and Parmigiano-Reggiano® in equal parts. Some include potatoes or green beans with the noodles. Pesto, now often made in blenders, also flavors minestrone.

A pungent garlic and vinegar sauce called aggiadda or agliata goes with soups and baccalà. Beyond basil, parsley, rosemary, marjoram and thyme, cooks use a mix of wild herbs called preboggion—which includes borage, chervil, chicory and other greens in season—to flavor pasta and soup. Other pastas include a type of ravioli called pansòuti, dumplings called fregamài and testaroli, small, round or figure-eight stamps known as

Genoa (Genova) is the administrative center of Liguria, whose other provinces are Imperia, La Spezia and Savona. The region ranks 18th in size (5,421 square kilometers) and 11th in population (1,633,000).

65

corzetti, the lasagne-like picagge and the thinner mandilli de saea (silk handkerchiefs).

Chickpea flour and olive oil make a tasty tart called farinata—or panissa when made with onions and fried. Here torta (cake) is rarely sweet. Torta pasqualina and torta verde are laden with vegetables, torta marinara with fish. Bread usually comes in rolls or as focaccia with oil, onions or cheese. The region has its own pizza dell'Andrea (after the heroic Admiral Andrea Doria) with onions, garlic, tomatoes, black olives and anchovies—or with sardines as sardenaira.

There's also a sweet pizza among Liguria's desserts, which range through ring-shaped biscuits called canestrelli, fried pastries called böxie (little lies), apple and raisin fritters called friscieu, Genoa's Easter fruitcake pandolce and the chestnut-pine nut tart called castagnaccio.

Seafood restaurants along the Riviera offer sea bass, prawns, scallops, oysters, lobsters and on occasion cappon magro ("lean capon," the wittily ironic name of a monumental salad that contains plenty of fish but no fowl). Coveted are gianchetti or bianchetti (larval anchovies and sardines available only briefly each year) and datteri (date-shells so rare that fishing is banned). Yet housewives rely on mussels, squid and other humble fish for soups called buridda and ciuppin. Recipes abound for anchovies and sardines (fresh or preserved), the dried tuna (or, in the past, dolphin) called mosciame and dried cod baccalà and stoccafisso.

The resourceful use of meat in the diet relies on the versatility of veal in roasts and stews, the breast loaf called cima ripiena, the rolled filets called tomaxelle, fried skewers called stecchi and as a source of tripe. Rabbit is popular, braised or stewed, as are poultry and lamb. Liguria produces little cheese, though Parmigiano-Reggiano®, pecorino, fresh ricotta and the acidic curds called prescinseua are prominent in cooking.

The region's olive oil known as Riviera Ligure is protected by a DOP. Ligurians prize their limited sources of wine, first among them the white from the seaside terraces of Cinque Terre, either dry or sweet as Sciacchetrà. Cinque Terre lies in the Riviera del Levante to the east of Genoa, where the Colli di Luni zone is noted for fine white Vermentino. The Riviera del Ponente to the west offers white Pigato and Vermentino and red Rossese di Dolceacqua and Ormeasco, from the Dolcetto grape.

DOP PRODUCT
Olive oil: Riviera Ligure.

SPECIALTIES OF LIGURIA

buridda Genoese soup of various fish in stock with plenty of garlic, anchovy, tomato.

cappon magro layers of garlic-rubbed sea biscuits, cooked vegetables, eggs and at least a dozen types of fresh fish form a mound crowned by oysters and lobsters.

capponada the poor man's cappon magro includes biscuits and mainly preserved fish.

cima ripiena veal breast stuffed with vegetables, eggs, herbs, pistachios and cheese.

ciuppin the humblest of fish stewed with tomato, garlic, onions, white wine and eaten as soup thickened with stale bread.

coniglio alla carlona rabbit braised in white wine with black olives, pine nuts, capers, herbs.

gianchetti all'agro the miniature fish served raw or poached with lemon, oil, parsley.

mes-ciua chick-peas, beans, farro and olive oil blend in an antique soup of La Spezia.

pansòuti con la salsa di noci pasta envelopes filled with ricotta and the preboggion bouquet of herbs, topped with walnut sauce and grated Parmigiano-Reggiano®.

sbira or sbirra tripe with tomatoes, potatoes and herbs served over slabs of toasted bread with Parmigiano-Reggiano®, eaten by Genoa's stevedores and sbirri (cops) after a day's work.

siluri torpedoes, the nickname for totani or flying squid, stuffed with cheese, breadcrumbs and garlic and stewed with wine and tomatoes.

stecchi fritti wooden skewers of various pieces of veal coated with thick batter that includes artichokes, mushrooms and grated cheese and fried in olive oil.

stocchefisce accomodou dried cod cooked with pine nuts, olives, mushrooms, potatoes, vegetables, herbs and anchovies, in white wine and tomato sauce.

tomaxelle veal rolls with a filling of mushrooms, pine nuts, breadcrumbs and eggs braised in tomato sauce.

torta pasqualina Easter tart based on artichokes or chard, hard-boiled eggs, ricotta and herbs, originally baked in 33 layers of dough.

Piedmont (Piemonte)

Piedmontese uphold their heritage of food and wine with unequaled staunchness. Turin, as the home of the Savoy dynasty that reigned as Italy's royal family, shared a culinary savoir faire with neighboring France. But the noblest examples of the good tastes of the past are to be found in the substantial cooking of the hill country.

The flavors of Piedmont reach peaks in autumn, when the harvest is in and wooded slopes from the Alps to the Apennines supply game, mushrooms and white truffles, whose magical aromas enhance pastas and risottos, meats and cheeses. Those foods call for full-bodied red wines, notably Barolo, Barbaresco and Barbera.

Piedmont's range of antipasti is so vast and varied that it represents a compendium of regional cooking with dishes that elsewhere might qualify as main courses. Classic openers are fonduta (cheese fondue), insalata di carne cruda (marinated raw beef), finanziera (a bizarre meat stew), vitello tonnato (veal with tuna sauce) and bagna caôda ("hot bath" for raw vegetables). Salads may consist of greens, asparagus, sweet-sour onions, beans or wild mushrooms. Red and yellow bell peppers are eaten with dressings or, like other vegetables, blended in flans called sformati. Zucchini flowers or Savoy cabbage (verza) leaves with meat-cheese fillings may be called caponet. Rice and cheese are used for croquettes, cakes and fritters. Eggs may be fried sunny side up with truffles or cooked with vegetables or peppers as frittata or in an onion custard called tartrà.

Antipasto lists continue with tongue, tripe, fried pig's trotters called batsoa (silk stockings), tonno di coniglio (marinated rabbit tender as tuna) and stewed snails. Pâtés and terrines are made of liver and game birds. Fine pork salumi include salame alla douja (aged in lard in earthenware vases) and blood sausages called sanguinacci. Salami is also made from beef, goose, trout and potatoes. Munched with virtually everything are grissini, yard-long breadsticks first baked in Turin in the 17th century.

Pastas are dominated by slender, hand-cut noodles called tajarin and ravioli-like envelopes called agnolotti, which take to different forms, fillings and sauces. Flatlands near the Po around Vercelli and Novara are Europe's leading suppliers of rice, notably the prized Carnaroli for risotto cooked with beans and pork as panissa or paniscia or with frogs, vegetable or meat sauces or simply with butter and shaved truffles. Polenta and potato gnocchi are favored in places, as are

68

Turin (Torino) is the administrative center of Piedmont, whose other provinces are Alessandria, Asti, Biella, Cuneo, Novara, Torino, Verbano-Cusio-Ossola and Vercelli. The region ranks 2nd in size (25,399 square kilometers) and 5th in population (4,288,000).

hearty soups, such as cisrà, with chickpeas and pork rind, and tòfeja, with beans, corn flour, vegetables and pork.

The region raises prized beef of the breed known as razza piemontese, eaten raw or braised in red wine, roasted, grilled or simmered as the base of bollito misto. Recipes abound for veal, lamb, kid and rabbit, as well as duck, goose, chicken, capon and pigeon. Pheasant, partridge, hare and venison are favorites among game. Meats and other items combine in Italy's most ambitious fritto misto. Fried pork liver is the base of a dish called griva. Tapulone is a stew of donkey meat served around Novara. Anchovies and tuna flavor many a dish, though fresh fish is secondary in the diet, with an exception for trout from mountain lakes and streams.

Piedmont produces quantities of Gorgonzola from Novara, as well as Taleggio and Grana Padano, DOP cheeses that are also made in neighboring regions. Piedmont also offers an intricate array of local cheeses protected by DOP. Notable are the soft Robiola di Roccaverano (based on sheep's milk) and Murazzano (based on cow's milk with some goat or sheep's milk blended in). The little wheels of Toma Piemontese originate in hill towns around the region. Tome or tume are usually based on cow's milk, as is the rare Castelmagno, sharp in flavor and flecked with blue mold. Bra, named for the town near Cuneo, may be soft when young or hard with age. The similar Raschera comes from the heights of the Maritime Alps. A pervasively pungent fermented cheese is known variously as bròs, bruss, bruz. Fontina, preferably from Valle d'Aosta, is widely used in cooking.

Piedmont is a major producer of hazelnuts, protected under IGP. They are used in pastries, cakes, chocolates and the nougat called torrone. Chestnuts are roasted or candied as marrons glacés. Among a wealth of biscuits, pastries and desserts, standouts are corn flour (meliga) cookies, the chocolate or coffee flavored custard cake called bonèt, cream cooked with caramel as panna cotta, an opulent chocolate cake called torta gianduia and fluffy zabaione, which supposedly originated here.

Piedmont boasts the greatest number of classified wines, with 9 DOCGs and 43 DOCs, including the region-wide appellation of Piemonte to classify premium wines. The Nebbiolo grape is the source of the regal Barolo and Barbaresco, though it also makes aged reds in the northern towns of Gattinara, Ghemme and Carema. Popular reds are Barbera and Dolcetto. Notable whites are the dry Gavi and Arneis and the sweet, bubbly Asti Spumante and its relative Moscato d'Asti. Turin is the world capital of vermouth, fortified wine flavored with herbs and spices.

69

DOP PRODUCTS
Cheeses: Bra, Castelmagno, Gorgonzola, Grana Padano, Murazzano, Raschera, Robiola di Roccaverano, Taleggio, Toma Piemontese.
Meat products: Salamini Italiani alla Cacciatora.

IGP PRODUCTS
Meat products: Mortadella Bologna.
Produce: Nocciola del Piemonte.

SPECIALTIES OF PIEDMONT
agnolotti al burro e salvia envelopes with a lean meat-herb filling served with fresh sage leaves sautéed in butter and grated Parmigiano-Reggiano®.
bagna caòda olive oil, butter, garlic and anchovies are the "hot bath" in an earthenware vessel into which raw cardoons, carrots, celery, fennel, cauliflower, jerusalem artichokes, spring onions and sliced bell peppers—among other items—are dipped.
brasato al Barolo beef marinated in Barolo with onions, carrots and herbs, braised to exquisite tenderness.
finanziera stew or sauce of veal brains, sweetbreads, chicken livers

and cockscombs and mushrooms stewed with garlic, vinegar and Marsala, though recipes vary.

fonduta Fontina cheese melted with butter, milk and egg yolks and worked with a whisk into a creamy mass topped with shaved white truffles.

fritto misto piemontese or fricia this deep-fried banquet includes lamb, chicken, veal, liver, brains, sweetbreads, pig's feet, sausages, artichokes, cauliflower, zucchini, mushrooms, apples, pears, cheese, dumplings, almond biscuits, though possibilities don't stop there.

gnocchi alla bava potato dumplings with butter, Fontina and grated Grana Padano.

grande bollito misto piemontese various cuts of beef and veal, including tongue and head, simmered with hen, cotechino sausage, onions, celery, carrots and served with bagnet verde (sauce of parsley, garlic, anchovy, breadcrumbs) or bagnet ross (peppery hot and red from tomatoes).

insalata di carne cruda finely chopped raw beef or veal marinated briefly in olive oil, garlic, lemon juice, served with salad greens or, in season, shaved truffles.

lepre in civet or sivè hare marinated and cooked with its blood, herbs, spices and red wine, sometimes confused with lepre in salmì, cooked without blood and served with strained gravy.

panissa risotto tinted with Barbera, braised with reddish borlotti beans, pork rind and salame alla douja, typical of Vercelli; paniscia of nearby Novara is subtly different.

polenta cùnsa cornmeal mixed with Fontina and toma, topped with butter and grated grana.

tajarin con i tartufi the noodles boiled in beef broth are flavored with melted butter, grated grana and a touch of nutmeg and topped with shaved truffles.

trota alla salvia brook trout braised in white wine and vinegar with bay leaf and fresh sage.

zabaione or zabaglione egg yolks whipped with sugar and Marsala into a delicious cream, which also flavors ice cream and semifreddo.

Valle d'Aosta (Vallée d'Aoste)

Italy's smallest region is tucked into the loftiest corner of the Alps with borders on France and Switzerland, neighbors who influence the cooking of the French-speaking population. Still, though Valle d'Aosta shares traditions with Piedmont (of which it was long a province), the foods of its Alpine valleys have rarefied character of their own.

Pasta and olive oil are novelties in a robust cuisine based on cheese and meat, rye bread, potatoes, polenta, gnocchi, rice and soups. Cows grazed in Alpine meadows provide fine butter and cheese called toma, Robiola and above all Fontina DOP, which figures in many a dish, including fondua, made with milk as in Piedmont's fonduta. Also DOP is Valle d'Aosta Fromadzo, a firm cow's milk cheese (sometimes with a bit of ewe's milk) that has been made in the valley since the 15th century. Cheese is also used with polenta, risotto and in thick soups, whose ingredients range beyond the usual vegetables, meat, rice and potatoes to include mushrooms, chestnuts and almonds.

Meat specialties are the beef stew called carbonade and breaded veal cutlets or costolette. Game abounds on the wooded Alpine slopes: partridge, grouse, hare, venison, as well as chamois and ibex (for which hunting is limited). Noted pork products are prosciutto called Jambon de Bosses, which rates a DOP, as does the Lard (salt pork) from the town of Arnad. Spicy blood sausages called boudins and salame are preserved in pork fat. Mocetta is the rare prosciutto of chamois or ibex. A curiosity is tetouns, cow's udder salt-cured with herbs, cooked, pressed and sliced fine like ham. Also prized is the trout that abounds in mountain streams.

The Alpine climate lends flavor to berries and fruit, especially apples and pears called martin sec that are cooked with red wine as dessert. The region is noted for fragrant mountain honey, almond biscuits called tegole and butter crisps known as torcetti.

The Valle d'Aosta (Vallée d'Aoste in French) regional DOC covers a broad range of wines made in strictly limited quantities. Such curios as the red Torrette and Enfer d'Arvier and the white Muscat de Chambave and Blanc de Morgex (from continental Europe's highest vineyards) need to be sampled locally.

Meals conclude with the passing of the grolla, a pot containing caffè valdostana (coffee with red wine, grappa and lemon peel), which is sipped from numerous spouts.

Aosta is the administrative center and lone province of Valle d'Aosta, which ranks 20th among the regions in both size (3,264 square kilometers) and population (120,000).

DOP PRODUCTS
Cheeses: Fontina, Valle d'Aosta Fromadzo.
Meat products: Jambon de Bosses, Valle d'Aosta Lard d'Arnad.

SPECIALTIES OF VALLE D'AOSTA
capriolo alla valdostana venison stewed in red wine with
vegetables, herbs, grappa, cream.
carbonade salt-cured beef cooked with onions and red wine in
a rich stew.
costoletta alla valdostana breaded veal cutlet with melted
Fontina and, in season, truffles.
minestra di castagne e riso thick soup of rice cooked in milk
with chestnuts.
polenta alla rascard cornmeal cooked, cooled and sliced,
then baked with layers of Fontina and a ragout of beef and
sausage.
risotto alla valdostana Fontina, toma, Parmigiano-Reggiano®
and butter make this one of the creamiest of rice dishes.
seupa à la valpellinentze soup of Savoy cabbage, rye bread,
Fontina, ham, salt pork, herbs and spices in beef broth.
seupa de gri barley soup with potatoes, onions, seasonal
vegetables, salt pork.

Lombardy (Lombardia)

Lombardy honors its richly diversified culinary heritage with dishes that are often elaborate and esoteric in taste. Milan's gastronomic traditions differ—if more in form than in substance—from the dining customs of the provinces in a territory that extends from the Alps along the lakes of Garda, Iseo, Como and Maggiore across the Po plains to the Apennines.

Provincial cooking merits individual attention, yet regional patterns of eating do show recurring themes. Risotto and polenta still surpass pasta in popularity. The habitual use of butter, cream and lard has only gradually yielded to olive oil in recipes.

Lombardy's popular cheeses are firm Grana Padano, blue-veined Gorgonzola, soft, ripe Taleggio, soft, mild Quartirolo Lombardo and tangy Provolone Valpadano, all covered by DOP, as well as creamy Robiola and Stracchino.

Lombardians are resolute consumers of meat and poultry (especially duck, goose and turkey). Beef is the base of bollito misto, eaten everywhere. The many recipes for veal include vitello tonnato, with tuna sauce, shared with Piedmont. Pork's customary utility extends through a range of salame, though salame also comes from beef and geese.

The pleasures of eating in old Milan were illustrated by Giuseppe Arcimboldo, a painter who used foods to create human likenesses. In Italy's rice capital the saffron-tinted risotto alla milanese is served with ossobuco (braised veal shank). Rice (or ris) is cooked in many ways: with erborinn (parsley), spàrgitt (asparagus), rape (turnips), rane (frogs) and coràda (calf's lung). The city's soups include robust minestrone and busecca (based on tripe). Noted meat dishes are costoletta alla milanese (breaded veal cutlet), casoeùla (pork stew), fritto misto (of veal brains, liver, lungs and sweetbreads) and mondeghili (meat croquettes). Milan is known for fine-grained pork salame that was traditionally made in the city, as well as in the nearby Brianza hills, where it rates a DOP. Panettone, a fluffy fruit cake, is a national Christmas institution.

To the south lies Pavia and the rice paddies near where the intricate risotto alla certosina was created at a Carthusian monastery. Pavia is known for zuppa alla pavese, risòtt rustì (rice with pork and beans), dishes with frogs, crayfish and snails, and the original colomba pasquale, the Easter cake in the form of a dove. Fine salume is made in the hills of Oltrepò Pavese, notably the Salame di Varzi, which rates a DOP. The town of Mortara is noted for goose salame, which rates a DOP, and fegato

Milan (Milano) is the administrative center of Lombardy, whose other provinces are Bergamo, Brescia, Como, Cremona, Lecco, Lodi, Mantova, Pavia, Sondrio and Varese. The region ranks 4th in size (23,861 square kilometers) and 1st in population (9,029,000).

grasso (foie gras).

Cremona, on the Po, is renowned for mostarda (mustard-flavored candied fruits) served with platters of bollito misto. Although the city may have been the birthplace of ravioli, its most noted pasta today is marubini, disks filled with meat and cheese and eaten in broth. A local treat is torrone, nougat based on almonds.

Como's Alpine lake supplies prized persico (perch), tiny fish called alborelle, which are fried and eaten whole, and agoni, dried and preserved with bay leaf as missultitt, eaten like sardines. Other delicacies are fitascetta (pastry with red onions), polenta vûncia (with garlic, butter and Grana Padano) and miascia (bread pudding with apples, pears, raisins and rosemary).

The Valtellina, near the Alpine border of Switzerland, is the home of the popular bresaola (air dried beef that rates an IGP) and violino (smoked goat prosciutto). Buckwheat (grano saraceno) is used for a cheese and grappa fritter called sciatt, as well as for noodles called pizzoccheri, for polenta in fiur (cooked with milk) and polenta taragna (with butter and the rare scimudin cheese). The valley's legendary cheese is the rustic Bitto DOP, though Valtellina Casera is also protected.

The provinces of Bergamo and Brescia share a ravioli-like pasta called casônsei and polenta e osei, with little birds cooked crisp enough to eat bones and all. That dish used to be so popular that it inspired a cake of the name with birds sculpted in almond paste. In the Taleggio valley near Bergamo the finest cheese of the name is ripened in caves. Formai de Mut dell'Alta Val Brembana comes from the Alpine valley north of Bergamo. Brescia's menus offer riso alla pitocca (rice boiled with chicken) and pike, tench and eel from the lakes of Garda and Iseo. Bagoss is an artisanal grana cheese from the village of Bagolino.

Mantua (Mantova) in the eastern flatlands is noted for pasta called agnolini, cooked with a rich beef-pork filling and tortelli envelopes stuffed with pumpkin. Vialone Nano rice is grown locally for risotto alla pilota (with sausages). Polenta is topped with ground salt pork as gras pistà. Mantua's many desserts include crescent pastries called offelle and cakes called bussolano (with potatoes and lemon) and the crumbly torta sbrisulona. Pears from Mantova are protected by an IGP. Part of the Parmigiano-Reggiano® DOP zone is in the province of Mantova.

Although the region produces little olive oil, two types rate DOP: Laghi Lombardi and Garda, from the shores of the lake.

Lombardy is not a large producer of wines when compared to neighboring Piedmont, Veneto and Emilia-Romagna. Yet some of its wines are growingly distinguished. Three rate as DOCG: Franciacorta, a sparkling wine made by the classical method of fermentation in bottle, and two reds from Nebbiolo grown in the Alpine Valtellina: Valtellina Superiore and Sforzato or Sfurzat, produced from semidried grapes. Notable among Lombardy's 14 DOCs are those of Oltrepò Pavese, which takes in a range of reds, whites and sparkling wines, and Lugana, a fruity white from vineyards to the south of Lake Garda.

DOP PRODUCTS
Cheeses: Bitto, Formai de Mut dell'Alta Valle Brembana, Gorgonzola, Grana Padano, Parmigiano-Reggiano®, Provolone Valpadana, Quartirolo Lombardo, Taleggio, Valtellina Casera.
Olive oils: Garda, Laghi Lombardi.
Meat products: Salame Brianza, Salame di Varzi, Salame d'Oca di Mortasa, Salamini Italiani alla Cacciatora.

IGP PRODUCTS
Meat products: Bresaola della Valtellina, Cotechino Modena, Mortadella Bologna, Zampone Modena.
Produce: Pera Mantovana.

SPECIALTIES OF LOMBARDY

busecca or büsêca soup of tripe with salt pork, diced salame, vegetables, herbs, grated grana.

casoeûla cuts of pork, sausage and rind stewed in wine with cabbage and herbs and eaten with polenta.

casônsei ravioli filled with sausage, bread and cheese in Brescia—and with those ingredients and more around Bergamo—always dressed with butter and Grana Padano.

costoletta alla milanese large veal cutlet with the bone, breaded, fried in butter and served with a sprinkling of lemon.

nervetti in insalata gristle from pig's foot and shank cooked tender with onions, carrots and celery and served as salad with vinegar and oil.

ossobuco alla milanese veal shank (cut across the bone to expose the marrow) braised in wine and herbs and flavored with gremolada (chopped parsley, garlic, grated lemon rind).

polenta e osei cornmeal shaped in a mound and topped with small birds (larks, thrush, warblers) spit roasted with sage leaves.

polenta pasticciata cooked cornmeal, sliced and baked with layers of tomato, pork and mushroom sauce.

rane in guazzetto frogs cooked with butter, onions, garlic, tomato, white wine.

risotto alla certosina rice braised with onions, peas, leeks and tomatoes, served with frog legs, filets of perch, crayfish and mushrooms.

risotto alla milanese the golden rice flavored with saffron, butter and grated Parmigiano-Reggiano® is traditionally eaten with ossobuco.

tacchina ripiena Christmas roast turkey stuffed with chestnuts, apples, pears, walnuts, minced veal, salt pork, brandy and herbs.
torta sbrisulona crisp crumb cake with corn meal, butter and almonds.

tortelli di zucca envelopes with a filling of yellow squash, mostarda, almond biscuits and cheese, served with butter and grated Parmigiano-Reggiano®.

uccelli scappati chunks of veal and pork skewered with sage

leaves and cooked to resemble "escaped birds."

vitello tonnato thin slices of roast or braised veal served cold with a creamy sauce flavored with tuna, capers, anchovy and lemon—though recipes vary.

zuppa alla pavese fresh eggs atop slices of bread fried in butter are poached and eaten in beef broth with grated Grana Padano.

Veneto

Venetian cooking has known exotic touches since the days when crusaders, merchants and adventurers such as Marco Polo opened trade routes to the east, providing Europe with coffee, tea and novel grains, herbs and spices. Still, though foods may be rich, varied and sometimes bizarre, Veneto boasts an enviably balanced diet from an eclectic range of sources.

The Adriatic abounds in fish. The plains of the Po, Adige and Piave rivers supply livestock, rice for risotto and corn for polenta. The hills that flank the Alps from Lake Garda to Cortina d'Ampezzo provide game, mushrooms, wine and a bit of olive oil, along with the climate for aging prosciutto, salame and cheeses. Gardens everywhere furnish fresh vegetables, notably the radicchio species of endive of Treviso and Verona.

As a seafood haven, Venice exalts risotto nero (blackened with cuttlefish ink), scampi (prawns) and spider crabs called granseole—or moleche when males shed their shells in spring and fall. Venetians have their own lexicon for creatures from the lagoon: cannolicchi or cape longhe (razor-shell clams), peoci (mussels), garusoli (spiky murex sea snails), cape sante and the smaller canestrelli (scallops), folpetti (curled

octopus), schile (tiny shrimp) and sardele (sardines). But Venetians also dine on the earthly likes of risi e bisi (rice and peas), fegato alla veneziana (calf's liver and onions) and Carpaccio. That raw beef dish originated in Venice, as did the rampantly fashionable dessert called tiramisù.

Cured pork products include variations on salami called soppressa or soppressata, as well as cotechino and other types of sausage. Around Vicenza, Soppressa Vicentina rates a DOP, as does the prosciutto from the Berici and Euganei hills in the southern Veneto. Cheeses singled out for DOP include Asiago, from Alpine meadows, and Monte Veronese, from the Lessini hills north of Verona, as well as Grana Padano, Montasio, Provolone Valpadana and Taleggio, shared with other regions.

Rice has always found greater favor among Venetians than pasta. The compact Vialone Nano from Verona's lowlands rates an IGP. It excels for risotto, or risoto, usually made by sautéeing the rice and base ingredients then simmering them in broth without stirring. Rice dishes, often substantial, include an endless variety of meat, fish, game, vegetables, mushrooms, herbs and odd combinations such as riso con

---

Venice (Venezia) is the administrative center of the Veneto, whose other provinces are Belluno, Padova, Rovigo, Treviso, Verona and Vicenza. The region ranks 8th in size (18,391 square kilometers) and 6th in population (4,488,000).

i bruscàndoli (wild hop shoots) and risi in cavroman (mutton spiced with cinnamon).

Special handmade pastas are the spaghetti-like bigoli, the ravioli-like cassunziei and the tagliatelle-like paparele. Noodles of all types go with beans in pasta e fagioli (fasioi in dialect)—the prime example of a range of soups made with rice, meat, fish and vegetables. The red beans of Lamon in the valleys around Belluno have IGP status.

The versatile radicchio rosso is used for salads, cooked in risotto and soups or grilled with oil and lemon as a separate dish. IGP status has been reserved for Radicchio Rosso di Treviso and Radicchio Variegato di Castelfranco. Also prized is the white asparagus of Bassano del Grappa and Cimaldomo, where it rates an IGP. Olive oils rate DOP

under Veneto, the regional appellation, and Garda, from the shores of the lake and Verona's hills.

Polenta can be a primo, though it's more often part of the main course, as a mush or grilled with meat dishes such as pastissada, stew made with beef or with horsemeat as pastissada de caval in Verona. There pearà, a sauce of beef marrow, grated bread and pepper is served with the ubiquitous bollito misto. Polenta accompanies duck, goose, guinea fowl, turkey (sometimes cooked with pomegranate) and game—such as wood pigeon, thrush, duck—dressed with peverade (sauce of chicken livers, salame, anchovies, oil, garlic, vinegar). Polenta also goes with carpione (salmon trout found only in Lake Garda), with stewed bisati (eels from the river deltas) or with dried cod called baccalà (but really stoccafisso), renowned from Vicenza.

The region's pastries and desserts include baicoli (sugar biscuits), zaleti (cornmeal-raisin cookies), fritole (fritters, with candied fruit and nuts for Carnival) and crema fritta (fried cream custard). Popular beyond the region are Verona's golden pandoro Christmas cake, the crumbly torta sabbiosa and fregolotta (with almonds) plus, of course, tiramisù.

Veneto has become the largest producer of wine among the 20 regions, as well as the leader in volume of classified DOC/DOCG. Verona's province is a prodigious producer with three DOCGs—Bardolino Superiore, Soave Superiore and the sweet Recioto di Soave. The popular red Valpolicella DOC appellation takes in the opulent Amarone, made from semidried or passito grapes. Vineyards elsewhere proliferate in Merlot and Cabernet, often drunk young, and white Pinots and Chardonnay. Bubbly white Prosecco is preferred by Venetians for frequent sipping of the little glassfuls they call ombre.

DOP PRODUCTS
Cheeses: Asiago, Grana Padano, Montasio, Monte Veronese,
Provolone Valpadana, Taleggio.
Meat products: Prosciutto Veneto Berico-Euganeo, Salamini
Italiani alla Cacciatora, Soppressa Vicentina.
Olive oils: Garda, Veneto.
Produce: Marrone di San Zeno.

IGP PRODUCTS
Meat products: Cotechino Modena, Mortadella Bologna,
Zampone Modena.
Produce: Asparago Bianco di Cimadolmo, Ciliegia di Marostica,
Fagioli di Lamon della Vallata Bellunese, Radicchio Rosso di
Treviso, Radicchio Variegato di Castelfranco, Riso Vialone Nano
Veronese.

SPECIALTIES OF THE VENETO
baccalà alla vicentina dried cod cooked in milk with onions,
anchovies and Grana Padano.
bigoli co l'anara "spaghetti" and sauce of duck liver and
innards with vegetables and herbs.
Carpaccio the original (named for the Venetian Renaissance
painter) was thin-sliced raw beef dressed with mayonnaise
containing mustard and Worcestershire sauce, though popularity
has inspired creations with meat, fish, cheese, mushrooms and
truffles.
fegato alla veneziana calf's liver sautéed with onions, parsley
and sage in butter and oil with a hint of vinegar.
granseola alla veneziana the meat of boiled spider crab
pounded in a mortar and served in the hollowed shell with olive
oil, pepper, lemon, parsley.
pasta e fasioi noodles of any type and beans in a thick
minestra, often flavored with onion, carrot, celery, pork rind,
though recipes vary around the region.
pasticcio di polenta layers of fried polenta and stew of wood
pigeon with mushrooms baked in pie crust.

pastissada de caval horsemeat stewed with tomatoes, onions
and herbs in red wine.
risi e bisi fresh peas sautéed in butter with onion, pork and
parsley, then simmered with rice in broth to the consistency of a
thick soup, served with grated Grana Padano.
risotto alla sbirraglia spring chicken and lean veal braised
with rice and vegetables.
risotto primavera diced string beans, artichokes, tomatoes,
carrots and potatoes united with peas and asparagus tips and
braised with rice in the spring.
sardele in saor sardines fried in oil with onions and flavored
with vinegar, marinated with pine nuts, raisins and lemon peel
and eaten as antipasto.
sopa coada pigeon sautéed with wine, vegetables, herbs, boned
and baked in a casserole with slices of bread laden with Grana
Padano and enough broth to make it a soup.
tiramisù coffee-flavored cream of mascarpone and eggs,
layered with savoiardi (ladyfingers) and topped with curls of bitter
chocolate.
torresani allo spiedo pigeons roasted on the spit with salt
pork basted with oil containing mashed bay leaf, rosemary,
juniper berries.

Friuli-Venezia Giulia

In this attractively secluded region where the Alps almost touch the Adriatic, the homespun cooking of the Friulian hill country presented historical contrasts with the more refined Venetian-style fare eaten along the coast. Over time, though, the two cuisines have reached a happy union in dishes accented—often rather sharply—by the tastes of Austrian and Slavic neighbors, who remember Trieste as their gateway to the Mediterranean.

In Alpine Carnia and the vine-draped hills of Udine and Gorizia, the open-hearth fogolar with conical chimney is used for grilling beef, lamb, kid, poultry, sausages and mushrooms. The indispensable polenta goes with cheese, meat stews, blood puddings and game: hare and venison often cooked in salmì (highly seasoned wine sauce) and a mixed flock of fowl, including woodcock, duck and little birds called uite.

Friuli's pride is the exquisite prosciutto of the town of San Daniele, which rates a DOP, though there are also sausages called lujanie and muset (the local cotechino), the neck cut called ossocollo and the smoked ham of Sauris. From mountain meadows come Montasio DOP cheese (the base of crisp frico) and ricotta called scuete, also smoked and aged for grating.

The ingredients for Friuli's medley of soups include pork, tripe, turnips, cabbage, corn, barley, mushrooms and above all fasùj, small reddish beans that also go with rice or noodles. Breads, beyond the usual wheat, are made from rye and barley flour as well as pumpkin.

Pastas include flakes called flics, tubes called sivilots and the curious cjalçons, envelopes with sweet-sour fillings for which various recipes include spinach, rye bread, raisins, candied fruit, potato, parsley, mint, brandy, chocolate and cinnamon.

Along the Adriatic between Lignano Sabbiadoro and Trieste recipes favor seafood: turbot, sardines, prawns, cuttlefish, squid, scallops, crabs, eels and even turtles cooked in soup. Chowder from the fishing port of Grado is called boreto alla graisana. There are several recipes for salt cod baccalà and many for risotto with fish, vegetables, herbs or frogs.

Trieste harbors eastern traditions in gulasch or gùlas (peppery beef stew), cevàpcici (grilled patties of minced pork and beef), rambasici (meat filled cabbage rolls), bòbici (soup with ham, beans, potatoes, corn kernels), potato gnocchi or gnocs made with plums or pumpkin.

Trieste is the administrative center of Friuli-Venezia Giulia, whose other provinces are Gorizia, Pordenone and Udine. The region ranks 17th in size (7,855 square kilometers) and 15th in population (1,184,000).

Pastas include lasagne with poppy seeds, the ravioli-like bauletti (with cheese-ham filling) and offelle (filled with spinach, veal, pork, onion). Wursts, sauerkraut and horseradish add to the tangs of Central Europe.

So do desserts, such as presnitz (rolls with raisins, nuts, candied fruits), strudel (pastry with apples, raisins, pine nuts, cinnamon) and a local version of the latter called strukli with potatoes in the dough and ricotta in the filling. Potatoes also go into crescent-shaped chifeleti biscuits. Other treats are pumpkin fritters called fritulis, chestnut cookies called castagnolis and the fluffy cake roll gubana.

Production of extra virgin olive oil has been revived around Trieste with the DOP of Tergeste.

Some of Italy's most prestigious white wines come from the hills of Collio Goriziano and Colli Orientali del Friuli: Tocai Friulano, Sauvignon, Chardonnay, Pinot Grigio, Pinot Bianco and the sweet Picolit and Verduzzo. Eminently drinkable are the red Merlot and Cabernet and wines from such local varieties as Pignolo, Schiopettino and Refosco. A sweet wine from the Verduzzo grape made at a place called Ramandolo is Friuli's lone DOCG. Here the tradition of grappa, or sgnape, is bolstered by production of the Slovenian plum brandy called slivovitz.

80

DOP PRODUCTS
Cheese: Montasio.
Meat products: Prosciutto di San Daniele, Salamini Italiani alla Cacciatora.
Olive oil: Tergeste.

SPECIALTIES OF FRIULI-VENEZIA GIULIA

boreto alla graisana chowder of fish (preferably turbot) stewed with olive oil, garlic, vinegar.

fasûj e uardi bean and barley soup with pork, onion, celery and herbs.

frico aged Montasio grated, mixed with cornmeal and fried flat and crisp; some recipes add chopped onions or potatoes.

granzevola alla triestina spider crab meat baked with breadcrumbs, garlic, lemon, parsley.

gubana yeast cake rolled around a filling of nuts, raisins, candied orange and lemon peels, bits of chocolate and cinnamon.

gulasch or gùlas beef stewed with onion, tomato, herbs, chili peppers and paprika.

jota or jote beans, potatoes and sausages simmered with broth in an earthenware pot are flavored with sauerkraut and sage sautéed in garlic in the Trieste version of the soup.

muset e bruada pork-rind sausage boiled and served with bruada or brovada (turnips pickled in vinegar), sautéed with onion, garlic, salt pork.

paparot corn meal with chopped spinach and garlic in a tasty gruel.

risotto di Marano rice boiled in fish stock served with sautéed shrimp, squid and mussels.

Trentino-Alto Adige

Amid the towering Dolomites of this northernmost region, Latin and Germanic cultures mingle but don't always mix. In Alto Adige (or Südtirol, the German-speaking province of Bolzano), Austro-Tyrolean cooking prevails with wursts, cabbage, potatoes, rye bread and dumpling soups. In Trentino (the province of Trento to the south), Italo-Venetian traditions of polenta and pasta take on Alpine accents with butter, cheese, game and wild mushrooms.

By now, though, many recipes are shared. South Tyroleans may dine on pizza or spaghetti as readily as Trentini eat crauti (sauerkraut) or canederli (the bread dumplings called Knödeln in German).

Trentino thrives on polenta, usually made from corn but also from potatoes or buckwheat, which is used in a sort of cake called smacafam, baked with sausage, salt pork and sometimes cheese. Beyond conventional ravioli and tagliatelle, first courses include bigoi (similar to the Veneto's bigoli) and strangolapreti ("priest strangler," gnocchi of spinach, flour, eggs and cheese).

Soups may contain tripe, pork, various vegetables, potatoes and turnips. Cornmeal and wheat flour with milk and butter make an ancient gruel called trisa—or Mus in Alto Adige. Along with recipes for dried cod stoccafisso, omelets and frittate, comes a selection of meats: poultry, rabbit, pork, blood sausages called biroldi and salt-cured beef called carne salata.

Alto Adige's gastronomic pride is Speck, boned pork flank smoked and aged by artisans, mainly in the Venosta valley. Speck dell'Alto Adige, which rates an IGP, is eaten as an opener or snack sliced or cubed with wedges of dark Bauernbrot or with crisp rye flatbread.

Knödeln, which often contain bits of liver or Speck, also come in a dark version with rye bread, buckwheat flour, leeks and bacon. Both may be served in broth or dry to accompany meats and vegetables. Popular soups contain barley and tripe. Sausage called Hauswurst is served with sauerkraut, pickles and horseradish. Noodles called Spätzli often go with beef dishes, such as peppery Rindsgulasch and Sauerbraten, pot roast with onions, wine and vinegar. From the lofty wilds come brook trout, venison and rare chamois and mountain goat.

Trento's prominent cheese is Grana Trentino, though Grana Padano DOP and Asiago DOP are also produced in the province, as is the locally prized Spressa delle Giudicarie DOP. Every Alpine village makes its own cheese called nostrano (ours). Alto Adige's many local

Trento (Trent) is the administrative center of Trentino-Alto Adige, whose other province is Bolzano (Bozen). The region ranks 11th in size (13,607 square kilometers) and 16th in population (930,000).

cheeses include the grainy, sharp Graukäse, soft, mild Pusteria and Pustertaler and goat's milk Ziegenkäse.

The region is Italy's leading producer of apples, which appear in strudel and the fritters called Apfelküchel. The apples of the high valley in Trentino are protected as Mela Val di Non DOP.

Zelten is a rye flour Christmas cake with candied fruit, nuts, honey, cinnamon and liqueur, though recipes vary between provinces. Krapfen are baked or fried pastries with jam. Trentino's sweet version of buckwheat smacafam contains raisins, nuts and aniseed.

The region, which exports a major share of its wine, classifies about 75 percent as DOC. Much of the production comes under the province-wide appellations of Trentino and Alto Adige, which each apply to numerous types and varieties of red, white, sweet and sparkling wines. Trento DOC applies exclusively to bottle-fermented sparkling wine, primarily from Chardonnay. Classic red wines with separate appellations are Kalterersee (or Caldaro) and St. Magdalener (Santa Maddalena) in Alto Adige and Teroldego Rotaliano in Trentino. Native red varieties of note are Lagrein and Vernatsch in Alto Adige and Marzemino and Teroldego in Trentino. Cabernet, Merlot and Pinot Nero also do well here. But the regions has gained a modern reputation with whites that reach fragrant heights in the Alpine air as Gewürztraminer, Sylvaner, Müller Thurgau, Sauvignon and the Pinots and Chardonnay that also make first-rate sparkling wines.

DOP PRODUCTS
Cheeses: Asiago, Grana Padano, Provolone Valpadana, Spressa della Giudicarie.
Olive oil: Garda (Trentino in part).
Produce: Mela Val di Non.

IGP PRODUCTS
Meat products: Mortadella Bologna, Speck dell'Alto Adige.

SPECIALTIES OF TRENTINO-ALTO ADIGE
biroldi con crauti blood sausages stuffed with chestnuts, walnuts and pine nuts, flavored with nutmeg, cloves and cinnamon, served with sauerkraut.
Blau Forelle trout poached in white wine with vinegar, lemon, bay leaf and clove, served with melted butter.
carne salata beef marinated for a month or more in brine with juniper berries, pepper and herbs, eaten either sliced raw or cooked in butter and served with beans or polenta
Gemsenfleisch chamois Tyrolean style with red wine vinegar, salt pork, herbs and sour cream served over toasted country bread.
orzetto or Gerstensuppe barley soup with onion, garlic, vegetables and herbs simmered with Speck—eaten in both provinces.
Leberknödelsuppe dumplings of bread crumbled and mixed with flour, milk and eggs and flavored with chopped calf's liver and herbs served in broth.
minestra di trippa Trento's tripe soup with onion, carrot, celery, garlic, potatoes, grated bread and tomato sauce.
Sauresuppe Tyrolean tripe soup with onion, herbs and nutmeg soured by white wine

Glossary

Commonly used Italian terms for food and beverages are defined here. The names of dishes and foods often differ from region to region. Local dishes and dialect terms for foods such as pastas, soups, cheeses, fish, meats, breads and desserts are given in regional chapters.

A

Acciuga or Alice - anchovy.

Aceto - vinegar; aceto balsamico tradizionale traditional balsamic vinegar (see in Emilia-Romagna).

Acqua minerale - mineral water, gassata bubbly, naturale still.

Affettati - sliced salumi (salame, prosciutto, etc.) or other meats, cold cuts.

Affumicato - smoke cured, as in meat, fish.

Aglio - garlic.

Agnello - lamb. Milk-fed lamb is called abbacchio in Rome and environs.

Agrodolce - sweet-sour or bittersweet.

Albicocca - apricot.

Amaretto - liqueur of bittersweet almond flavor used for amaretti biscuits.

Amaro - bitter taste, also bitter liqueur, usually based on herbs.

Ananas - pineapple.

Anatra or Anitra - duck.

Anguilla - eel.

Animelle - sweetbreads.

Antipasto - appetizer or pre-meal course; antipasti cover a miscellany of raw, cooked or pickled vegetable, meat and fish dishes, salads, cheeses, canapés, fritters and tarts.

Aperitivo - aperitif, pre-meal drink.

Arancia - orange; aranciata orange-based soft drink.

Arrosto - roast, normally meat cooked in an oven or on a spit or grill.

Asparago - asparagus.

Astice - lobster; aragosta is spiny Mediterranean rock lobster.

B

Baccalà or Bacalà - salt-dried cod, base of popular recipes throughout Italy; often synonymous with wind-dried stoccafisso (see).

Barbabietola - beet or beetroot.

Basilico - basil.

Bergamotto - bergamot, a citrus fruit whose oil is used for flavoring and in perfumes.

Besciamella - béchamel, white sauce based on milk or cream.

Bevanda or Bibita - beverage or drink.

Bietola - chard.

Bignè - pastry puff or fritter, often filled with sweet creams, sometimes with cheese.

Birra - beer. Birreria is a brewery or a place that serves beer.

Biscotti - biscuits or cookies; biscottini are tiny types.

Bistecca - beef steak, though the term also applies to veal or pork chop.

Bitter - English term used for beverages of bitter flavor.

Bocconcini - bite-sized morsels, as in stews or fried tidbits of meat or cheese.

Bollito - boiled; b... misto mixed simmered meats, also called lesso.

Bottarga or Buttariga - eggs of mullet or tuna dried firm and sliced over pasta or salad.

Braciola - cutlet or chop of pork, veal, lamb; in southern Italy bracciola or brasciola may refer to a stuffed roll of meat or fish similar to involtini (see).

Brandy - English term used to describe a spirit distilled from aged wine.

Brasato - braised, usually beef cooked in red wine.

Bresaola - air dried filet of beef, specialty of Alpine Lombardy.

Brioche - light pastry roll or bun; various types include the croissant of French origin, also called cornetto.

Broccoletti - broccoli, but curiously broccoli in Italian refers to various cabbage family sprouts or leaves, including turnips and cauliflower.

Brodetto or Brodeto - soup or chowder, usually made with fish in many versions along the Adriatic Sea.

Brodo - broth or stock from boiled meats, vegetables or fish.

Budino - pudding, originally sweet, though molds or purées of rice, vegetables or meat may use the name.

Bue - beef from fully mature male cattle or oxen (see manzo, vitellone).

Burro - butter.

C

Cacciagione - game procured by hunting (caccia), distinguished as c... da pelo (furry) and c... da penna (feathered). See selvaggina.

Cacciatore - hunter; alla cacciatora refers to hunter's style stews or sauces.

Cacio - ancient term for cheese, still in use as a synonym for sheep's milk pecorino and other types from goats and cows, such as caciocavallo in the south and caciotta in the center.

Caffè - coffee; c... espresso is thick and strong from steam forced under pressure through fine grounds; espresso is the base of c... macchiato (with a dab of frothy steamed milk) and cappuccino or cappuccio with more frothy milk; c... latte contains still more milk.

Calamari - squid; calamaretti are tiny squid often confused with seppie or cuttlefish.

Calzone or Pizza ripieno - pizza dough folded over a filling and baked or fried.

Cannella - cinnamon.

Capperi - capers.

Cappone - capon, rooster castrated to heighten flavor of meat.

Capretto - kid.

Caprino - goat's milk cheese.

Capriolo - roebuck or venison; cervo, the once prized stag, is rare.

Caramello - caramel or other candy; caramellizzato

84

caramelized or glazed.

Carciofo - artichoke.

Cardo - cardoon, a thistle similar in taste and texture to artichoke; also called gobbo.

Carne - meat.

Carote - carrots.

Cassata - Sicilian cake, also popularly ice cream covered with a chocolate shell.

Castagna - chestnut; marrone is the largest and most prized version.

Castrato - mutton.

Cavolfiore - cauliflower.

Cavolo - cabbage; c... verza Savoy cabbage; cavolini di Bruxelles brussel sprouts.

Ceci - chickpeas.

Cena - supper or dinner; see pranzo.

Cervello - brain, veal and lamb brains may be cooked in various ways.

Cetriolo - cucumber.

China - quinine, used in liqueur called china and to flavor beverages described as chinato.

Chiocciole - snails, also called lumache (see).

Chiodi di garofano - cloves.

Cicoria - chicory, both cultivated and wild, as well as its relative endive, ranging from white cicoria di Bruxelles (Belgian endive) to green-speared catalogna (asparagus endive) to radicchio. See indivia, radicchio.

Ciliegie - cherries; amarene and marasche are bitter varieties.

Cinghiale - wild boar.

Cioccolato - chocolate.

Cipolla - onion; cipolline or cipollette small or spring onions; erbe cipolline chives.

Colazione - lunch or morning snack; prima colazione breakfast; see pranzo.

Clementina - clementine, small orange citrus fruit.

Conchiglie - generic term for hard-shelled mollusks (clams, mussels, scallops, etc.); conchiglia di San Giacomo pilgrim scallop, also known as cappasanta or ventaglio.

Condimenti - condiments, from condire (to season or dress); the term covers a vast range of sauces and flavorings.

Confettura - jam, also called marmellata, which originally meant citrus fruit marmalade.

Coniglio - rabbit.

Contorno - side dish or garnish, usually vegetables or salad.

Costata - rib steak of beef or veal, also called tagliata.

Costoletta - cutlet or chop of pork, lamb or veal, synonymous with cotoletta, the popular term for breaded veal cutlet.

Cotechino - large pork sausage traditionally containing rind or cotica, hence the name.

Cotto - cooked; ben cotto well done.

Cozze - mussels; also called mitili, muscioli, muscoli, peoci.

Crema - pastry cream or other viscous substance, also custard, cream soup. Dairy cream is panna.

Crescione - cress; crescione d'acqua watercress.

Crespelle - crepes, sometimes sweet but usually served with fillings or sauces like pasta.

85

Crosta - crust; crostata fruit tart; crostino crouton or toast with a spread.

Crostacei - crustaceans, such as shrimp, lobster, crabs.

Crudo - raw.

Cucina - kitchen (also stove or range); cooking, cookery, cuisine.

Cuoca/Cuoco - cook; in restaurants often known as lo chef.

D

Dattero - date; dattero di mare sea date or date-shell mollusk.

(Al) Dente - "to the tooth" for pasta cooked to proper firmness.

(Alla) Diavola - "devil's style" referring to hot seasoning or cooking over red hot coals, as with grilled chicken called pollo alla diavola.

Digestivo - after dinner drink, such as amaro or liqueurs, said to aid digestion.

Dolce - sweet; dolci cover pastries, cakes and other sweets of the course also known in Italian as dessert.

Dragoncello - tarragon or estragon.

E

Erbe - herbs; erbe aromatiche are scented types, such as basil, rosemary, sage, thyme and parsley; erbe selvatiche are wild.

Espresso - express; see caffè.

F

Fagiano - pheasant.

Fagioli - beans, specifically shelled varieties—such as white cannellini or reddish borlotti—cooked freshly shelled (sgranati) or often dried.

Fagiolini - green (or yellow) beans in their pods, notably string beans.

Faraona - guinea fowl or hen.

Farina - flour, from wheat as well as other grains, nuts and legumes.

Farro - ancient grain, predecessor of hard wheat, used in soups, breads, polenta.

Fava - fava or broad bean.

Fegato - liver; f... d'oca foie gras; fegatini di pollo chicken livers, fegatelli pieces of pork liver.

Fico - fig; f... d'India is the edible fruit of prickly pear cactus.

Filetto - fillet or filet of meat, fish.

Finocchio - fennel; f...selvatico or finocchiella is wild fennel, whose seeds and green leaves are used as seasoning.

Fiore - flower; fiori di zucca or zucchini squash flowers; fior di latte cow's milk mozzarella.

Focaccia - flat bread made in many styles, usually salty, sometimes sweet.

Fonduta - fondue.

Formaggio - cheese. Various types are described in Italian Specialty Foods and regional chapters.

Formaggio di fossa - cheese of sheep or cow's milk in forms wrapped in cloth and buried in pits where mold forms during fermentation which accounts for sharp flavor.

Forno - oven or bakery; al forno baked or roasted in the oven; fornaio baker.

Fragola - strawberry; f... di bosco or selvatica is the wild type.

Frantoio - mill where olives are processed for oil.

Frittata - eggs mixed with vegetables, meat or cheese and fried like a thick pancake on both sides. See omeletta.

Frittelle - fritters or pancakes, often with sweet ingredients but also meat or cheese.

Fritto - fried; f... misto mixed fried foods.

Frutta - fruit.

Frutti di mare - assorted seafood, chiefly mollusks and crustaceans, raw or cooked.

Funghi - mushrooms.

G

Gambero - name used for various crustaceans; g... rosso and g... imperiale or mazzancolla are large Mediterranean prawns, also called gamberoni; gamberelli are smaller prawns, gamberetti tiny shrimp; g... d'acqua dolce freshwater crayfish.

Gastronomia - gastronomy; gastronomo or buongustaio gourmet, ghiottone glutton.

Gelato - frozen dessert, such as ice cream or sherbet, of wide-ranging flavors, chiefly fruit, nuts and chocolate.

Ginepro - juniper, whose berries are used as seasoning.

Gnocchi - dumplings from potato and flour or semolino, usually served dressed as a first course; g... verdi are green from spinach mixed with ricotta; gnocchetti are smaller.

Grana - hard cow's milk cheese of grainy texture, notably Grana Padano, Parmigiano-Reggiano®.

Granchio - crab of various types; the large granciporro is prized; grancevola or granzeola is spider crab.

Granita - slushy gelato made by freezing liquid—often coffee or lemon juice—into crystals of grainy texture.

Grano - grain; g... duro durum wheat; g... saraceno buckwheat; granturco or maìs corn.

Grappa - spirit distilled from pomace of grapes previously crushed for wine; usually clear but sometimes amber from wood aging.

Griglia - grill; terms for grilling over coals include alla griglia, ai ferri, alla brace; grigliata mista mixed grill of meats or seafood.

Grissini - breadsticks.

Guanciale - salt pork from the cheek or jowl.

Gusto - the sense of taste; gustoso tasty.

I

Indivia - endive; i... riccia and scarola (curly and broad-leafed escarole), i... belga (Belgian endive, also called insalata belga or cicoria di Bruxelles). See cicoria, radicchio.

Insaccati - generic term for salumi (see) encased in membrane or other coverings.

Insalata - salad, popular examples are i... mista (mixed), i... verde (greens only); i... russa (mixed cooked vegetables diced with mayonnaise).

Involtini - envelopes or rolls of thinly sliced veal, pork or fish cooked with stuffing.

L

Lampone - raspberry.

Lardo - fat cut of pork from the lower back, salt cured with herbs and spices and consumed raw sliced with bread. Lard is called strutto (see).

Latte - milk; latticini dairy products.

Lattuga - lettuce, covering a range of types.

Lauro - laurel or bay, also called alloro.

Lenticchie - lentils.

Lepre - hare.

Limone - lemon; limonata lemonade; limetta or limone bergamotto lime, limoncello lemon liqueur.

Lingua - tongue.

Liquori - liqueurs; the term covers the range of distilled spirits, such as grappa and brandy, and compositions, such as amaro, limonello and sambuca.

Locanda - inn, ancient term for a simple place with rooms, often serving meals; today synonymous with osteria or trattoria.

Lombata - loin of beef, veal or lamb; lombo is pork loin.

Lumache - snails, distinguished as l... di terra (land varieties) and l... di mare (sea); both are also called chiocciole.

M

Maccheroni - macaroni; in parts of southern Italy maccheroni is a generic term for dried pasta, though elsewhere it usually refers to short pasta tubes.

Macedonia - mixed fresh fruits, a dessert.

Macelleria - butcher shop, macellaio butcher.

Maggiorana - marjoram.

Maiale - pork.

Mandarino - mandarin, a tangerine like the larger mandarancio and smaller clementina.

Mandorla - almond; mandorlata means containing almonds or their flavor.

Manzo - beef from adult male or female cattle, though younger than bue (see).

(Alla) Marinara - mariner's style, usually referring to dishes with tomato sauce.

Marinata - marinade.

Marzapane - marzipan, sweet almond paste, used in pastries; also called pasta reale.

Mascarpone - lightly fermented cream whipped smooth; unsweetened it may be used in pasta or risotto, sweetened with fruit or desserts.

Mazzancolla - large prawn also called gambero imperiale.

Mela - apple; mela cotogna quince.

Melanzane - eggplants or aubergines.

Melone or Popone - cantaloupe or muskmelon; watermelon is cocomero or anguria.

Menta - mint; many species, wild and cultivated, are used in cooking and beverages; m... piperita peppermint; mentuccia is a tasty variety popular in Rome.

Merenda - snack, light meal or picnic, also called spuntino.

Miele - honey.

Minestra - generic term for soup and also for first course (covering pasta, risotto, gnocchi, etc.); minestra in brodo broth with pasta or rice; minestrone vegetable soup; minestrina light soup or broth. See zuppa.

Mitili or Muscioli or Muscoli - mussels, also called cozze.

Molino - flour mill.

Molluschi - mollusks, including octopus, squid and shellfish, such as clams and mussels.

Mortadella - large pork sausage, originally of Bologna.

Mostarda - candied fruit flavored with mustard seed, specialty of Cremona. See senape.

Mozzarella - smooth, soft white cheese originally from milk of water buffalo (bufala), though cow's milk fior di latte may

88

also use the name.

N

Nettarina - nectarine, also known as pesca noce.

Nocciola - hazelnut.

Noce - walnut; the plural noci is the generic term for nuts; n... di cocco coconut; n... moscata nutmeg; noce also refers to rumpsteak of beef or veal; noce di burro is a knob of butter.

Nocino - bittersweet liqueur made with green walnuts in their husks.

Norcineria - butcher shop specializing in pork and salume; norcino pork butcher.

O

Oca - goose.

Olio - oil, comestible types include o... di arachide (peanut), girasole (sunflower), mais (corn), noce (walnut), semi vari (seeds).

Olio di oliva - olive oil. See Italian Specialty Foods for an explanation of quality and types. Olives are also cured for eating and used in cooking.

Omeletta - omelet, beaten eggs cooked thin and folded, often over a filling of vegetables, cheese, meat or fish. See frittata.

Origano - oregano, herb from dried marjoram leaves.

Orto - vegetable garden; ortaggi fresh garden produce.

Orzo - barley, used mainly in soups but also toasted and ground as a coffee substitute.

Ossobuco - cut of veal shank exposing the bone and its marrow-filled hollow.

Osteria - simple tavern serving local wine and often food, though the name sometimes applies to fancier places.

Ostriche - oysters.

P

Pancetta - cut of pork or veal from the belly or lower rib. The pork is often salt cured and eaten sliced raw or cooked; when smoked it is p... affumicata or bacon.

Pane - bread; also written pan and applied to cakes, such as pan di Spagna (sponge cake).

Panino - bread roll, also when split and filled as a sandwich.

Panna - dairy cream; p... montata is whipped.

Parmigiano-Reggiano® - trade name of the cheese often known abroad as Parmesan; alla parmigiana refers to dishes cooked with the cheese.

Pasta - paste or dough, also the generic term for noodles and the like made from flour and liquid in two basic versions: p... secca (dried) and p... fresca (freshly made).

Pasta asciutta - cooked noodles served dry (asciutta), usually with sauce, as opposed to pasta in brodo, cooked in broth or soup; pastina small pasta used in soups; pastificio pasta factory.

Pasta filata - cheese made by "spinning" or stretching curds (pasta) into strands molded into spongy forms as in mozzarella or aged firm as in caciocavallo and provolone.

Pasticceria - pastry or pastry shop.

Pasticcio - baked composition of various ingredients, such as pasta, polenta, meat, vegetables, cheese.

Pasto - meal, repast. See also cena, colazione, pranzo.

Patata - potato.

Pecorino - sheep's milk cheese.

Pepe nero - black pepper; p... bianco (white) and p... rosso (red) are also common.

Peperoncini - hot red or green peppers, especially chili.

Peperoni - sweet or bell peppers, red, yellow or green.

Pera - pear.

Pesca - peach; p... noce nectarine.

Pescatore - fisherman; alla pescatora refers to fish sauces, usually on pasta or rice.

Pesce - fish. Many species and seafood dishes are described with regional foods.

Pesto - sauce or dressing whose ingredients are mashed with a pestle in a mortar, notably in p... genovese (see in Liguria).

Petto - breast, usually of poultry.

Piatto - plate or dish, also a course in the meal, such as primo p..., secondo p... or p... di mezzo. See explanation of meal terms under Eating in Italy.

Piccante - piquant or peppery flavor.

Piccione - pigeon; wild or wood pigeons are colombacci or palombacci.

Pignoli - pine nuts.

Pinzimonio - olive oil with salt, pepper and sometimes vinegar into which raw vegetables are dipped and eaten as salad or antipasto.

Piselli - peas; pisellini are small or baby peas.

Pizza - Naples' familiar flatbread is baked by pizzaioli in pizzerie everywhere, though toppings and cooking styles vary; alla pizzaiola refers to tomato-garlic sauce, not only for pizza but for pasta and meat.

Polenta - cornmeal boiled and eaten as a mush with sauce, gravy, butter, cheese or meat, or cooled and sliced to be fried or grilled; porridge-like pastes from buckwheat, farro (see) or chestnut flour may also be called polenta.

Pollame - poultry.

Pollo - chicken, gallo is cock or rooster, gallina hen; the free-range variety is p... ruspante; pollastro or galletto is a young chicken.

Polpetta or Polpettone - meatball or croquet of minced fish or vegetables; polpettone may also be meat loaf.

Polpo or Polipo - octopus; moscardino is the tiny curled octopus.

Pomodoro - tomato.

Pompelmo - grapefruit.

Porchetta - whole pig, boned, stuffed with herbs and roasted in a wood-burning oven; porchetto (also maialino or porcellino) is suckling pig.

Porro - leek.

Pranzo - lunch (synonymous with colazione) in parts of Italy, dinner or supper (synonymous with cena) in others; pranzo also refers to an important meal or banquet: p... d'affare business lunch or dinner; p... di nozze wedding banquet or feast.

Prezzemolo - parsley.

Prosciutto - ham, whether salt-cured crudo (raw), cotto (cooked) or affumicato (smoked). The term may also apply to a leg of wild boar, goat, goose or turkey.

Prugna - plum; p... secca prune.

Purè or Purèa - purée of vegetables or fruit; p... di patate mashed potatoes.

Q

Quaglia - quail.

R

Rabarbaro - rhubarb and also the liqueur made from it.

Radicchio - endive or chicory, best known as the red-leafed varieties of Treviso and Verona.

Rafano - horseradish, also called cren.

ragù - ragout or stewed or braised meat sauce.

Rana - frog, usually eaten fried or in risotto.

Rapa - turnip, whose greens are called cime di rapa.

Ravanello - radish.

Razza - ray or skate flatfish.

Ribes - currants, black, red or white.

Riccio di mare - sea urchin, eaten as frutti di mare and in sauces.

Ricotta - reheated, or "recooked" whey molded into a soft, white mound that may be eaten fresh or used in pasta fillings, gnocchi and pastries, though it may also be salted and dried for grating. Traditionally from milk of sheep or goats, it also comes from cows.

Ripieno - stuffing or filling for pasta, meat, vegetables.

Riso - rice; Italy grows many varieties for use in soups, salads, puddings, etc., though the prized varieties are for braised rice dishes called risotto. See Italian Specialty Foods for descriptions of types.

Ristorante - restaurant, Italy's top category of dining establishment.

Rognoni or Rognoncini - kidneys, lamb and veal are preferred.

Rosmarino - rosemary.

Rosticceria - shop or eating place specializing in roast meats and poultry. Sometimes called girarrosto, in reference to the large spit that typifies such places.

Rucola - salad green (Eruca sativa) resembling cress but with spicy, slightly bitter flavor. Also called arugula and rocket in English and often confused with sharper flavored wild ruchetta, which is prized in salads of field greens.

S

Salame - salami, covering many types and forms of preserved minced meats.

Salamoia - brine or salty solution in which foods such as olives, pickles, cheese, fish and meats are conserved.

Sale - salt, a fundamental flavoring and preserver of foods.

Salsa - sauce, covering a wide range of dressings and condiments.

Salsiccia - sausage.

Saltata or Saltato - sautéed.

Salume - generic term for salt-cured meat, such as salame, salsiccia, prosciutto, bresaola. See Salumi under Italian Specialty Foods. Salumeria shop where salumi are sold.

Salvia - sage.

Sambuca - liqueur of anice or licorice-like flavor based on wild elder (sambuco) flowers.

(Al) Sangue - cooked rare, usually beef.

Sapore - flavor or savor; saporito flavorful.

Sardine - sardines preserved in oil; fresh sardines are called sarde.

Scalogno - shallot.

Scaloppine - scallops or flattened slices of veal—also pork—often breaded and fried.

Scampi - prawns or jumbo shrimp; the term is used loosely in Italy.

Sedano - celery, also called accia.

Ségale - rye, used for bread and crackers mainly in Alpine areas.

Sella - saddle of lamb, veal, rabbit or venison.

Selvaggina - game procured by either hunting or breeding. See cacciagione.

Semifreddo - "partly frozen" dessert of soft ice cream or custard with meringue, fruit, mascarpone, zabaglione or cake.

Semola - coarse durum wheat flour used to make pasta as semola di grano duro; semolino (called semolina in English) is the finer flour used for pasta and gnocchi and in soups.

Senape - mustard, the condiment made from mustard seed, wine and vinegar, not to be confused with mostarda (see).

Seppia - cuttlefish, often confused with calamari (squid).

Sformato - mold of cooked and minced vegetables, also dessert similar to custard or flan.

Soppressa - minced pork "pressed" into form similar to a large salame in Veneto; soppressata refers to various types of salumi in Italy.

Sorbetto - sherbet or sorbet of soft texture based on fruit, sometimes with wine or spirits.

Sottaceto - foods preserved in vinegar, generally vegetables or mushrooms, pickles.

Sott'olio - foods preserved in olive (or other) oil, such as vegetables, mushrooms, tuna, sardines, anchovies, small cheeses, salami.

Spalla - shoulder of veal, lamb or pork, or pork shoulder salt-cured like prosciutto.

Speck - boned pork flank smoked and aged, a specialty of Alto Adige.

Spezie - spices.

Spezzatino - meat stew consisting of small pieces.

Spiedo - spit for roasting; spiedino skewer or brochette of meats or fish.

Spinaci - spinach.

Spremuta - juice of freshly squeezed fruit; succo is the generic term for juice.

Spumone - ice cream of foamy texture from mascarpone and beaten egg yolks.

Spuntino - snack or light lunch—also called snack in Italian.

Stoccafisso - stockfish, cod wind-dried on poles, also called pesce stocco or simply stocco or stocche; often synonymous with salt-cured baccalà.

Stracotto - beef braised long and slowly, similar to brasato.

Strutto - lard, rendered pork fat, not the same as lardo (see).

Stufato - meat, usually beef, stewed very long.

Sugo - sauce or gravy (also called intingolo), when based on cooked meat synonymous with ragù, often used with pasta.

T

Tacchino - turkey.

Tartufo - truffle, subterranean fungus prized as white Tuber magnatum (shaved raw over special dishes) and black Tuber melanosporum (eaten raw or preserved); t... di cioccolato chocolate truffle; t... di mare small clam.

Taverna - tavern, bar or inn serving drinks and sometimes meals.

92

Tavola or Tavolo - table; tavola calda shop or snack bar serving hot dishes.

Té - tea, made from dry leaves of the tea shrub and other plants; tè freddo iced tea.

Terrina - terrine, ceramic cooking vessel and the pâté or gelatin of meat, fish or vegetables cooked in it, usually served cool; t... d'anatra ai pistacchi duck and pistachio pâté.

Testa or Testina - head of beef, veal or lamb and its parts, usually used for salumi, though also prized in bollito misto (see).

Timo - thyme.

Tonno - tuna, eaten fresh or more often preserved in oil; tonnato refers to tuna-flavored sauce.

Tordo - thrush, the choicest of the little game birds known collectively as uccellini.

Torrone - nougat, candy from honey and whipped egg whites with almond and hazelnuts.

Torta - cake as well as tart or pie or focaccia, ranging over numerous sweets as well as torte salate, salty types with meat, cheese or vegetables.

Tramezzino - bread sliced and filled as a sandwich (the English term is a popular synonym).

Trattoria - unpretentious eatery, often family run, specializing in local cooking.

Trippa - tripe.

Trota - trout.

U

(In) Umido - meat cooked in dense liquid, including brasato, spezzatino, stracotto, stufato.

Uovo - egg; uova is plural.

Uva - grape; u... da tavola table grape; uva passa dried grape to be used for wine; uvetta, uva secca or sultanina are terms for raisin.

V

Vaniglia - vanilla.

Verdura - green-leafed vegetables, though the term refers to garden produce in general, including legumes and roots.

Vino - wine, v... da tavola table wine, vino da arrosto robust aged red wine suited to roast meats.

Vitella or Vitello - veal; vitellone beef from young cattle.

Vongole - small clams used mainly in pasta or soups, led by the preferred vongola verace (the "authentic" Venerupis decussata).

Z

Zabaione or Zabaglione - fluffy amalgam of egg yolks, sugar and wine (usually Marsala), eaten warm like a custard or with cake or in gelato or semifreddo.

Zafferano - saffron, the dried orange-red stigmas of the crocus flower.

Zampone - sausage encased in the skin of pig's foot (zampa).

Zenzero - ginger, though the term is used in Tuscany for hot pepper.

Zucca - squash, including pumpkin, whose pulp is used mainly as pasta filling; the smaller zucchine are called zucchini, marrows, courgettes; flowers of both are a fried delicacy.

Zucchero - sugar.

Zuppa - soup, covering a range of vegetable, bean, meat and fish-based recipes, in theory thicker than a classical minestra, though the division isn't always clear; z... inglese custard cake soaked in sweet wine or liqueur.

About the Italian Trade Commission

ICE, the Italian Institute for Foreign Trade, is the Italian government agency entrusted with the development, facilitation and promotion of trade between Italy and other countries in the world. Its mission is to support the internationalization of Italian firms and their consolidation in foreign markets. The Italian Trade Commission has a network of 111 offices in 84 countries, 6 of which are located in the United States, ICE is the most authoritative ambassador of Made in Italy excellence in the world. For more information visit **www.italtrade.com**

About the Author:

Burton Anderson, a native of Minnesota, is an internationally acclaimed authority on Italian wine. A former editor of the International Herald Tribune in Paris, he has lived in Tuscany for nearly 30 years writing about Italian wine, food and travel. He was awarded the "Targa d'onore e di merito" of the Italian Sommeliers Association as "the Italian wine personality most followed and credited abroad" and the "Gran Medaglia d'Argento di Cangrande".

Other books include:
Burton Anderson's Best Italian Wines
Diane Publishing Co. (2004)
Wines of Italy (pocket guide)
Mitchell Beazley (2004)
The Wine Atlas of Italy
Mitchell Beazley (1999)
Franciacorta, Italy's Sanctuary of Sparkling Wine
Giorgio Mondadori (1999)
Vino, the Wines & Winemakers of Italy
Atlantic-Little Brown Books (1980)